College Students IN TRANSITION

AN ANNOTATED BIBLIOGRAPHY

Stephanie M. Foote, Sara E. Hinkle, Jeannine Kranzow, Matthew D. Pistilli, La'Tonya Rease Miles, & Janelle G. Simmons

Cite as:

Foote, S. M., Hinkle, S. E., Kranzow, J., Pistilli, M. D., Rease Miles, L., & Simmons, J. G. (2013). College students in transition: An annotated bibliography. Columbia, SC: University of South Carolina, National Resource Center for The First-Year Experience and Students in Transition.

ISBN 978-1-889271-88-0
Published by:
National Resource Center for The First-Year Experience® and Students in Transition
University of South Carolina
1728 College Street, Columbia, SC 29208
www.sc.edu/fye

Production Staff for the National Resource Center:

Project Editor	Tracy L. Skipper, Assistant Director of Publications
Design and Production	Allison Minsk, Graphic Artist

Library of Congress Cataloging-in-Publication Data

Foote, Stephanie M.
College students in transition : an annotated bibliography / Stephanie M. Foote [and five others].
pages cm.
Includes bibliographical references and index.
ISBN 978-1-889271-88-0
1. College students--United States--Abstracts. 2. College sophomores--United States--Abstracts. 3. College seniors--United States--Abstracts. 4. Transfer students--United States--Abstracts. I. Title.
LA229.F575 2013
378.1'980973--dc23

2013026107

This book is dedicated to all college students in transition and the many faculty and staff who are committed to their academic and personal success.

About the Publisher

The National Resource Center for The First-Year Experience and Students in Transition was born out of the success of the University of South Carolina's much-honored University 101 course and a series of annual conferences focused on the freshman year experience. The momentum created by the educators attending these early conferences paved the way for the development of the National Resource Center, which was established at the University of South Carolina in 1986. As the National Resource Center broadened its focus to include other significant student transitions in higher education, it underwent several name changes, adopting the National Resource Center for The First-Year Experience and Students in Transition in 1998.

Today, the Center collaborates with its institutional partner, University 101 Programs, in pursuit of its mission to advance and support efforts to improve student learning and transitions into and through higher education. We achieve this mission by providing opportunities for the exchange of practical and scholarly information as well as the discussion of trends and issues in our field through the convening of conferences and other professional development events such as institutes, workshops, and online learning opportunities; publication of scholarly practice books, research reports, a peer-reviewed journal, electronic newsletters, and guides; generating, supporting, and disseminating research and scholarship; hosting visiting scholars; and maintaining several online channels for resource sharing and communication, including a dynamic website, listservs, and social media outlets.

The National Resource Center serves as the trusted expert, internationally recognized leader, and clearinghouse for scholarship, policy, and best practice for all postsecondary student transitions.

Institutional Home

The National Resource Center is located at the University of South Carolina's flagship campus in Columbia. Founded in 1805, USC Columbia's mission is twofold: to establish and maintain excellence in its student population, faculty, academic programs, living and learning environment, technological infrastructure, library resources, research and scholarship, public and private support and endowment; and to enhance the industrial, economic, and cultural potential of the state. The Columbia campus offers 324 degree programs through its 14 degree-granting colleges and schools. Students have been awarded more than $16.7 million for national scholarships and fellowships since 1994. In fiscal year 2012, faculty generated $238 million in funding for research, outreach, and training programs. Carolina is one of only 63 public universities listed by the Carnegie Foundation in the highest tier of research institutions in the U.S.

CONTENTS

FOREWORD

Higher education professionals have long been aware that students' developmental and educational experiences do not begin and end in the first college year. While the transition to college from high school can set an important precedent, it is only one of many steps in an educational trajectory; the sophomore year, transfer between institutions, and the senior-year experience all represent common and important milestones in the timeline for college students. There are also a host of important transitions that occur within each of these stages of progress through college, such as moving into on-campus housing or an off-campus living experience; changing majors or career interests; studying away or abroad; failing a class and learning to reach out for assistance; and forging, nurturing, and, sometimes, even ending relationships with peers, family, staff, or faculty. In addition, the college years can represent an important phase in an individual's lifelong process of identity development by providing accelerated and diverse opportunities for exploration, growth, and maturity with respect to one's sense of self and place in a larger community.

As evidenced by the annotations in this new volume, during the past few decades, there has been increased attention paid to transition experiences beyond the first year. While the work at the National Resource Center for The First-Year Experience and Students in Transition has historically been rooted in first-year programs and research, our interests, mission, and even our name ("Students in Transition" was added in 1995) have expanded to encompass these "other" transition experiences. The Center has refocused its efforts and resources to address the national interest in students at all transition points and to lead and drive the conversation around these other stages in the educational pipeline. Further, the unique experiences of special populations of students at each of these critical junctures are recognized as important to examine in the broader discussion of student transitions. Finally, while each of these transition points is important in its own right, they are also interconnected within the larger picture of student learning, development, and success. Ultimately, the Center strives to remain true to its core commitments, which include the belief that "student transitions ... are critical junctures in the educational pipeline and unique opportunities for post-secondary student learning and development [and] we strive to set a standard of excellence for supporting student transitions and facilitating educational success for a diversity of students in the 21st century."

Transition is synonymous with change, which is a constant force in our educational, personal, and professional lives. On a daily basis, educators are called upon to help students succeed in college by navigating change. In addition, the challenge and support that colleges and universities offer students during the critical junctures in their educational journey help them develop competencies and skills to manage transition throughout the rest of their lives. Therefore, it is crucial higher education professionals have a better understanding of student needs and concerns beyond the first year in order to create the necessary programs, policies, and pedagogies that support students during their entire academic careers as a foundation for these life skills. To that end, this volume attempts to broaden our knowledge by identifying contemporary research and literature that addresses the experiences of students in transition beyond just the first year of college.

Edited by a team of higher educators who are actively engaged in both scholarship and practice around student transition and success, this book (a) represents an intersection of research and practice, (b) is a collaboration among professionals with different academic roles, (c) leverages connections across academic and student affairs, (d) considers a range of disciplinary viewpoints, and (e) seeks to honor the diverse backgrounds and unique experiences of the students navigating multiple transition points in their journey through higher education. I would like to thank the editors of this book and the publications staff of the National Resource Center for lending their time, experience, analysis, and expertise to the project. We are pleased to add this volume to the Center's library of scholarly practice books and hope that it will serve as an important resource for practice; a catalyst for future research; a foundation for advocacy; and a source of inspiration for dialogue regarding the refinement and advancement of policy, pedagogy, and practice in support of all students in transition.

Jennifer R. Keup
Director
National Resource Center for The First-Year Experience and
Students in Transition
University of South Carolina

INTRODUCTION

The college experience comprises numerous transitions for students, which existing research describes as processes involving an event or nonevent resulting in changes in behaviors and relationships (Goodman, Schlossberg, & Anderson, 2006; Moos & Tsu, 1976; Schlossberg, 1981, 1984). While the transition to and through the first college year has been the subject of many studies and analyses (e.g., Koch, Foote, Hinkle, Keup, & Pistilli, 2007), less is known about the types of transitions students navigate following that early experience, such as changing (or failing) year levels, transferring between institutions, restarting a degree pathway, getting involved in cocurricular or extracurricular opportunities, or preparing for graduation. Although not as well documented, these other transitions can have a significant impact on student success. At the same time, the nature of a college education is changing, with students earning degrees composed of coursework from multiple institutions and a growing number of courses and degree programs offered partially or wholly online. From 2002 to 2012, the number of online students exceeded 6.1 million (Allen, Seaman, Lederman, & Jaschik, 2012). As the student population diversifies and pathways to and through higher education become increasingly varied (Tinto, 2012), the very nature of the transitions students experience are changing as rapidly as the students themselves.

Schlossberg's transition theory (Goodman et al., 2006) is a model for understanding how students experience transition and a framework for helping students navigate those experiences. The types of transitions she and her colleagues identified—anticipated or predictable (e.g., applying to graduate school), unanticipated (e.g., campus or personal tragedies), or nonevents (e.g., a rejected application)—make clear that the transitions students experience in college go well beyond simply joining a new academic community, advancing to upper-level study, or graduating. For this reason, in examining works to include in this collection, we defined transition as a point or period in which a student encounters an event or nonevent that may impact his or her progression toward educational or personal goals.

While we can generate a standard list of transitions students are likely to experience as they move into, through, and out of higher education, Schlossberg's transition theory reminds us that transitions are unique to individual students. That is, the significance a student places on a transition depends on his or her relationship to the transition, its setting, (i.e., context), and the impact on daily life (as cited in Evans, Forney, Guido, Patton, & Renn, 2010). For example, a transfer student, veteran, and an international student may all face a transition to a new institution, but the context in which they approach that event can differ significantly, resulting in very dissimilar transition experiences. Lastly, how individuals respond to these transitions depends on variables or situation factors, such as timing, duration, previous experience with similar transitions, or concurrent stress (Goodman et al., 2006). These factors also account for the variability in responses when a type of transition is experienced multiple times. For instance, a college student may transfer several times during the course of his or her undergraduate career. Though the process of transferring might be familiar, how the student responds to each transition can be different depending on the unique situational factors of each institution.

The entries in this book describe studies on various points of transition in the college experience and populations of students who are considered to be in transition. It is beyond the scope of this volume to describe the characteristics of all the different types of college students in transition or the nuanced transitions they experience. Therefore, we have focused on the literature and research that has applicability to what we felt were some of the more common transition points beyond the first college year: (a) the sophomore year, (b) transfer from one institution to another, and (c) the senior year and transition out of college. We have also chosen to focus on several populations of students who have unique transitions into and through higher education. These include students who begin or return to higher education at a nontraditional age (e.g., adult learners and student veterans). We have also included a group we identified as student sojourners, those who are pursing higher education in a new country or culture (i.e., international and study abroad students).

As the nature of these transition points is constantly shifting to reflect changes in student demographics and institutional policies and procedures, we attempted to identify contemporary research (from approximately 2000 to present) for inclusion in this collection. The timeliness of the work was considered as well as how it represented the notion of transition as conceptualized by Schlossberg and her colleagues. In addition to annotating existing research, each chapter summarizes the key findings while highlighting omissions and areas for future research. It is our hope the readers of this book will help fill these gaps in our knowledge of college students in transition by conducting their own research and contributing to the literature base.

When we first began the journey of writing this book, we knew it would be a lengthy process because, in many respects, we were mapping uncharted territory. Culling research on transitions beyond the first year of college is a nuanced and complex process. For some of these students in transition, there are volumes of research; for others, the research is nascent or even nonexistent. There is much yet to be learned about who these students are, the types of transitions they experience, and how we can best support their success and retention. This collection represents an initial effort in broadening our understanding and suggesting new directions for research and practice in our work with college students in transition.

CHAPTER 1

The Sophmore-Year Transition

This chapter offers an overview of the literature focusing on the success of sophomore students in transition. While the emphasis of the early college years has historically been on the first year, practitioners and researchers have placed increasing attention on the second college year in the past 15 years amid concerns that sophomores were foundering once the supports of the first year were withdrawn. Yet, since the 1950s, educators have highlighted potential concerns about the second college year. Freedman (1956) characterized the sophomore year as a period of "inertia or disorganization" (p. 22), while Feldman and Newcomb (1969) noted a decline in satisfaction with the institution in the second year. In the mid-1980s, Lemons and Richmond (1987) identified doubts about career choice, dissatisfaction with relationships, and concerns about financing college as characteristics of the sophomore slump—a feeling of disconnectedness from the institution resulting in a drop in academic performance. Other hallmarks of the sophomore slump might include struggles with identify development; efforts to define personal beliefs, values, and interests; and challenges to set goals for college and beyond (Gardner, Pattengale, & Schreiner, 2000; Lemons & Richmond, 1987; Margolis, 1976). By the end of the sophomore year, students on most campuses will have to declare a major or may be faced with the need to change majors if they have not performed well in gateway courses. The need to make what is perceived as a high-stakes decision may lead to anxiety for some students.

Given the range of challenges students face in the second college year, intervention strategies in the areas of academic advising, career planning, and student engagement, as well as an understanding of student development and learning, can all contribute to the academic advancement and persistence of this population. As many institutions are discovering, for students to remain successful, learning, curricular and cocurricular linkages, collaboration across campus, and commitment to high-impact learning practices cannot decrease in the sophomore year. Rather, there must be an intentional commitment to ensure the level of institutional support for sophomores remains constant and consistent.

The chapter is divided into two sections. The first collects sources that have explored the nature of the sophomore transition and a range of initiatives designed to help students succeed in the second college year. Because indecision about major and/or career can put students at risk for withdrawal, much attention has been given to academic advising, major exploration, and career development in the sophomore year. Research and descriptions of initiatives focused on academic advising and career development have been collected into a second section.

Summary of Findings

Programs in advising and career planning are common, yet many transitioning sophomores appear to lack commitment, connectedness (to curriculum and/or community), and sense of purpose. An accumulation of credits without specific goals and direction can leave students struggling and feeling lost.

High-impact practices (e.g., undergraduate research, service-learning, writing-intensive courses, collaborative learning), which encourage student connections to faculty members and curricula, are critical for student success throughout the college experience. Without institutional intentionality, sophomores can drift away from learning goals, focusing more on socializing and activities that fail to encourage persistence and student engagement. Studies comparing students who participate in sophomore programs (of various cocurricular types) with those who do not show promise in terms of improved outcomes and persistence rates.

The limited literature on academic advising and career planning for first-generation sophomore students indicates that they can struggle academically even more than their second-generation peers. First-generation sophomore GPAs and self-efficacy scores have been found to be lower than those who are not first-generation.

Omissions and Areas of Future Research

While several substantial works focus on sophomore student initiatives and success, there is still much that is not understood. We identified fewer than 10 sources meeting our selection criteria published within the last decade. Compared to the plethora of research about the first year of college, there is an evident reduction in research interest on college sophomores. Yet, both qualitative and quantitative research on this population is critical if we are to meet the goals set by the Obama administration for college completion. The call for more empirical research on the sophomore transition issued by Gardner et. al (2000) more than a decade ago appears to have gone largely unanswered.

Notably sparse is research on first-generation sophomore students and studies related to nontraditional sophomores. This is concerning since those two populations make up a substantial portion of those in higher education today. Future research might simply disaggregate, highlight, and report findings about sophomores who are often included as part of a larger data set or large-scale study. Another area for future research relates to sophomore student transition in different fields of study. It is possible that the sophomore experience varies notably from one major to another, but there is not sufficient research to make any conclusions.

Understanding and Supporting the Sophomore Transition

Graunke, S. S., & Woosley, S. A. (2005). An exploration of the factors that affect the academic success of sophomores. *College Student Journal, 39*(2), 367-376.

This study explored how sophomores' experiences and attitudes affected their academic success (measured by grade point average). It focused particularly on student-faculty interactions, involvement in activities, commitment to academic major, and commitment to the university. Participants were second-semester sophomores at a public university in the Midwest (*N* = 1,093) who completed a mailed survey. The findings indicated that neither involvement in activities nor institutional commitment were predictors of academic success; however, certainty of academic major and interactions with faculty were more significant and impactful. As students transition from taking general education classes to major courses, many may develop anxieties if they are uncertain about their major. The researchers recommended that institutions create sophomore-specific programs to help students find and commit to a major and facilitate the development of close relationships with faculty.

Kennedy, K., & Upcraft, M. L. (2010). Keys to success: A look at the literature. In M. S. Hunter, B. Tobolowsky, J. N. Gardner, S. E. Evenbeck, J. A. Pattengale, M. A. Schaller, L. A. Schreiner, & Associates, *Helping sophomores succeed: Understanding the second-year experience* (pp. 30-42). San Francisco, CA: Jossey-Bass.

This chapter described some of the existing research on sophomore student success and examples of institutional interventions that assist these students. Using Astin's I-E-O (input-environment-outcome) model, the authors examined several general keys to sophomore student success (e.g., student inputs, institutional characteristics, experiences both in and out of the classroom) and identified several challenges affecting academic performance, such as developmental concerns involving self-identity, major or career indecision, and dissatisfaction with the college experience.

The authors suggested these factors may contribute to the sophomore slump that some students experience. The chapter concluded with recommendations for institutional interventions to assist the academic development and engagement of sophomore students: specifically, creating opportunities for advising and undergraduate research.

Keup, J. R., Gahagan, J., & Goodwin, R. N. (2010). *2008 National Survey of Sophomore Initiatives: Curricular and cocurricular structures supporting the success of second-year college students* (Research Reports on College Transitions No. 1). Columbia, SC: University of South Carolina, National Resource Center for The First-Year Experience & Students in Transition.
This research report described national findings from the 2008 administration of a survey of 382 institutions that reported having sophomore programs and initiatives. The findings indicated that student retention, satisfaction, and engagement were the most common reasons for institutions to create programs for sophomore-level students. For the most part, the type of sophomore programs institutions reported most frequently were career planning, academic advising, leadership development, and class events. Although less frequent, the authors indicated that study abroad, service-learning, community service, and undergraduate research were important curricular approaches to engage students at the sophomore level. Implications for practice include creating curricular and cocurricular programs for sophomore student engagement and developing a comprehensive approach to assessing those programs and initiatives.

Nnadozie, E., Ishiyama, J., & Chon, J. (2001). Undergraduate research internships and graduate school success. *Journal of College Student Development, 42*(2), 145-156.
This study examined the relationship between participation of McNair Scholars (i.e., low-income, first-generation and/or underrepresented students) in an undergraduate research internship and success in graduate school. Success referred to students' ability to secure admission into graduate school and complete the graduate degree. Directors of the McNair Scholars Program nationally ($n = 35$) were surveyed and asked to report on various features of their respective programs (e.g., number and type of workshops offered). The study also measured the degree of rigor within each program. The findings suggested that undergraduate research internships appeared to be unrelated to graduate school placement. Further, the application processes were not particularly rigorous or demanding. Results also suggested that the internship itself was not sufficient to determine successful entrance and progress in graduate school. Based upon their experiences with the McNair

Program at Truman State University, the researchers surmised that preparation, presentation, and publication—especially in the sophomore year—were keys to a successful undergraduate research experience and, eventually, the transition to graduate school.

Schaller, M. A. (2005, July/August). Wandering and wondering: Traversing the uneven terrain of the second college year. *About Campus, 10*(3), 17-24.
This article reported on a qualitative study using one-on-one interviews and focus groups to better understand the challenges facing college sophomores. The participants in the study were 19 sophomore students attending a midsized, private, Catholic college. The findings revealed that sophomores move through four stages of development: (a) random exploration, (b) focused exploration, (c) tentative choices, and (d) commitment. Random exploration was used to describe the delayed decision-making processes and lack of self-reflection participants demonstrated. In contrast, during focused exploration, participants connected to their inner voices and began to question their personal choices. The author suggested that because this stage incorporated significant personal reflection, students who remained in the stage longer developed a more comprehensive view of their lives. The tentative choices stage involved making decisions that affected their college careers and was marked with doubt about early decisions. Finally, although most participants did not reach the commitment stage, the author indicated that those who did expressed confidence in their personal decisions. A central recommendation emerging from the study was the need for more reflection, particularly while students were in the random exploration stage. To facilitate this reflection, the author argued that institutions need to develop opportunities for experiential and exploratory learning, as well as additional supports to encourage these students to get in touch with who they are and what that means for them.

Schaller, M. A. (2010). Understanding the impact of the second year of college. In M. S. Hunter, B. Tobolowsky, J. N. Gardner, S. E. Evenbeck, J. A. Pattengale, M. A. Schaller, L. A. Schreiner, & Associates, *Helping sophomores succeed: Understanding the second-year experience* (pp. 13-29). San Francisco, CA: Jossey-Bass.
The chapter author identified issues and characteristics that affect the academic and social integration of sophomore students, beginning with a discussion of the development of and rationale for sophomore programs. Schaller argued that because first-year programs are so common, students in their second year might feel abandoned without any support structure to help them navigate this transition. Acknowledging a paucity of information about the differences between first-year

and sophomore students, the author suggests issues and characteristics (e.g., choosing a major; career development; academic self-efficacy; incongruence between values and personal interests, goals, or abilities; financial strain; faculty-student interactions; peer relationships; academic engagement; overall satisfaction) that emerge in the second year can directly affect the retention and success of these students. Personal characteristics involving gender, race and ethnic diversity, age, sexual orientation, and socioeconomic status also affect sophomores. It was recommended that all of the aforementioned factors be considered in the development of programs to assist sophomore students.

Schreiner, L. A., Miller, S. M., Pullins, T. L., & Seppelt, T. L. (2012). Beyond sophomore survival. In L. A. Schreiner, M. C. Louis, & D. D. Nelson (Eds.), *Thriving in transitions: A research-based approach to college student success* (pp. 111-136). Columbia, SC: University of South Carolina, National Resource Center for The First-Year Experience and Students in Transition.
This chapter drew upon the work of two studies investigating the sophomore experience to make recommendations supporting the success and transition of second-year students. The first study examined responses of 4,845 sophomores to the Sophomore Experiences Survey (SES). Findings indicated that the most important contributors to sophomore thriving included faculty interaction, a feeling of belonging on campus, and a sense of purpose in terms of major or career selection. Spirituality was also identified as a thriving predictor. In the second study, interview data collected from 23 students who scored in the highest and lowest deciles on the SES suggested that students who are highly engaged make connections with faculty and other students in their major, while those who are struggling to feel a part of the campus community often identify a sense of decreased institutional support from the first to second year. The authors suggested the following ways to support sophomore thriving: (a) arrange for sophomore-faculty interaction, (b) create a sense of community both inside and outside the classroom, (c) provide meaningful academic advising to help students reflect and move toward future goals, (d) nurture students' search for spiritual meaning, and (e) assess sophomore support mechanisms and institutional policies.

Tobolowsky, B. F., & Cox, B. E. (Eds.). (2007). *Shedding light on sophomores: An exploration of the second college year* (Monograph No. 47). Columbia, SC: University of South Carolina, National Resource Center for The First-Year Experience and Students in Transition.
Chapters in this edited collection covered information on the psychological, cognitive development, and transition theories related to sophomores; literature on the

sophomore slump; Schaller's four-stage transition model; and the results of the 2005 National Survey on Sophomore Initiatives. In addition, the book provided institutional examples of the initiatives reported in the survey and in a Sophomore Summit convened in 2006. The monograph culminated with a chapter guiding readers on how to adapt and use the described best practices. Specifically, faculty and staff involved with sophomore programming were encouraged to engage in campus audits and promote collaboration between student and academic affairs departments. Drawing on the findings from the 2005 National Survey and research on sophomore student transitions, the authors described curricular and cocurricular experiences (e.g., transition classes, learning communities, retreats, traditions) that might contribute to the success of sophomores. Finally, the authors recommended ways institutions can engage sophomores in purposeful curricular and cocurricular activities, including undergraduate research and major and career planning.

Vuong, M., Brown-Welty, S., & Tracz, S. (2010). The effects of self-efficacy on academic success of first-generation college sophomore students. *Journal of College Student Development, 51*(1), 50–64.

The investigators in this study examined the relationship between self-efficacy and academic success among first-generation sophomores. Data were collected from 1,291 sophomores (34% first-generation) from five California State University institutions, using subscales on the College Self-Efficacy Inventory (CSEI). Findings revealed significant differences between the GPAs of the participants who were first-generation students and those who were second-generation; however, differences in perceptions of self-efficacy between the two groups were not found. Further, the results supported other research suggesting personal perceptions about academic abilities influence overall performance and persistence. The investigators recommended that institutions become deliberate in their work to help students make connections among concepts they are learning and integrate that learning into other aspects of their lives.

Wilder, J. S. (1993). The sophomore slump: A complex developmental period that contributes to attrition. *College Student Affairs Journal, 12*(2), 18-27.

This study differentiated between two kinds of sophomore students: (a) decliners (i.e., achieved a 2.75-4.0 GPA during their first year and then declined by 20% the next two semesters) and (b) maintainers (i.e., earned a 2.75-4.0 GPA and then sustained or improved their grades over the next two semesters). The researcher sought to identify factors that differentiated these two groups by comparing approximately equal numbers of students in the study. Three instruments were used to collect data from the sample populations: (a) the Biodata Form, (b) the

Children's Academic Motivation Inventory-Revised (CAMI-R), and (c) the State Trait Anxiety Inventory (STAI). The 196 students (102 decliners and 94 maintainers) completed and submitted all three instruments, which were then scored, coded, and evaluated. The results indicated differences between decliners and maintainers in the areas of institutional commitment, goals, and interactions with faculty and staff. Also significant was that decliners were more likely to be absent from class and engaged in nonacademic activities. It was recommended that institutions develop early-alert systems to identify and monitor students who decline for two consecutive academic terms. Further, sophomore-specific programming, particularly advising, should be implemented to help students as they transition to their second year in college.

Academic Advising and Career Development

Anderson, E., & Schreiner, L. A. (2000). Advising for sophomore success. In L. A. Schreiner & J. Pattengale (Eds.), *Visible solutions for invisible students: Helping sophomores succeed* (Monograph No. 31, pp. 55-77). Columbia, SC: University of South Carolina, National Resource Center for The First-Year Experience and Students in Transition.

This chapter discussed the supports that sophomores need from an academic advising perspective. Sophomores have concerns that are ideally addressed within the academic advising setting. These include struggling with major choices, understanding the significance of general education, developing satisfying relationships with peers and faculty, and staying motivated to persist. The authors provided a literature review to discuss works in the area of advising and motivation. They offered specific examples and guidelines for ways that advising programs can meet the needs of sophomore students by including strategies to identify and address concerns, by planning for their future, and by encouraging participation in campus life and community.

Gardner, P. D. (2000). From drift to engagement: Finding purpose and making career connections in the sophomore year. In L. A. Schreiner & J. Pattengale (Eds.), *Visible solutions for invisible students: Helping sophomores succeed* (Monograph No. 31, pp. 67-77). Columbia, SC: University of South Carolina, National Resource Center for The First-Year Experience and Students in Transition.

This chapter describes a study that was intended to develop models of student skill and competency acquisition throughout the college years. Survey data from two different instruments were collected on 280 sophomores at a public university as part of a larger study ($N = 2{,}414$). Results indicated that as students transitioned from the first to the sophomore year, and from the sophomore to the junior and senior years, significant changes in terms of the degree of student engagement took place. Sophomores in the study drifted away from academic goals, did not take responsibility for their own learning, and spent less time in academic pursuits and more time socializing with peers than students in higher or lower class standings. The primary concerns of sophomore students pertained to decisions about major and career. The authors encouraged campuses to reflect on ways in which institutional structures could support engagement from the first year to the sophomore year. Additionally, campuses could evaluate whether service-learning, sophomore-level internships, on-campus jobs, and/or more integrated and intentional career service assistance would benefit their sophomore or drifting populations.

Gordon, V. N. (2010). Academic advising: Helping sophomores succeed. In M. S. Hunter, B. F. Tobolowsky, J. N. Gardner, S. E. Evenbeck, J. A. Pattengale, M. A. Schaller, L. A. Schreiner, & Associates, *Helping sophomores succeed: Understanding and improving the second-year experience* (pp. 83-98). San Francisco, CA: Jossey-Bass.

This chapter focused on the aspects of academic advising understood to be particularly relevant for sophomore students, as well as other issues that can impact student success and achievement for this population. Three key advising aspects discussed were major selection, academic planning, and readjusting to the campus environment. Other topics highlighted in the chapter included transfer issues, family situations, academic resources (e.g., sophomore seminars, orientations, information available through technology), the need to transition sophomores to their junior year as it approaches, and the importance of advisor training and development. During the sophomore year, many students declare or change majors, discover they are not well suited to the selected major, and question the decisions they have made. Advisors can be critical in facilitating a smooth transition for rising sophomores by encouraging students to reflect on their first-year experiences and successes, helping them understand their strengths and goals, assisting them with an academic plan, discussing opportunities (e.g., study abroad, internships), and suggesting participation in campus activities.

Gordon, V. N., & Steele, G. E. (1992). Advising major changers: Students in transition. *NACADA Journal, 12,* 22-27.

In this article, the authors described an academic alternatives advising program aimed at students who were earning academic credit but were not making sufficient progress toward a degree. Specifically, the students in this program were identified because (a) they did not meet academic benchmarks required for their chosen major, (b) they had upper-level status and had not declared a major, or

(c) they had been denied admission to their chosen major. Academic advisors in this program had a lower advising ratio compared to the advising load in other programs or areas of the college, engaged students in individual and group advising, and facilitated the academic alternatives course. Evaluation and assessment of the program indicated that some students who had participated were able to gain admission to the academic program to which they had initially been denied access and others had made progress toward the degree in a new major they declared during the program. A total of 13% of the participants failed to make satisfactory progress and were academically dismissed. The authors suggested that students changing from one major to another be considered students in transition, even if they were native students.

Gore, P. A., Jr., & Carter, L. P. (Eds.). (2011). *Students in transition: Research and practice in career development* (Monograph No. 55). Columbia, SC: University of South Carolina, National Resource Center for The First-Year Experience & Students in Transition.

The monograph includes a series of case studies describing assessed career development initiatives for students throughout the college years. Several of these focus on initiatives designed to support second-year college students. For example, Gettysburg College engaged first-year students and sophomores in a weeklong career immersion experience designed to help them gain first-hand knowledge of a particular career, gauge their fit with that career, and guide them in the career exploration process. Students reported gains in their understanding of career interests and goals, networking skills, knowledge of skills required for success in a particular career, ability to assess their personal career fit, and recognition of how background and experiences influenced career choice. Elon College offered a leadership program designed to help students develop their capacity for self-authorship as a way to support them with major decision making. Finally, the University of Richmond helped students focus on developing identity and purpose and connecting academic and career goals as part of a larger initiative designed to respond to concerns about high attrition rates among sophomore men. Program participants reported feeling less anxiety about academic planning and career decision making and were more likely to take advantage of support services on campus one year later. The case studies and essays on research strategies in this volume provide career development professionals with models for supporting career exploration among students in transition and testing the efficacy of those efforts.

Isakovski, T., Kruml, S. M., Bibb, J. F., & Benson, A. D. (2011). C-SCAPE: One business school's answer to the sophomore slump. ***Academy of Educational Leadership Journal, 15*****(4), 17-33.**

This article presented an integrated sophomore-year experience course (Career-scape or C-scape) designed to nurture millennial sophomore students and help them avoid the sophomore slump. The two-course sequence was offered to sophomore-level business majors at a comprehensive, Midwestern, liberal arts university with a high percentage of first-generation college students (40% or more). The business department collaborated with the university's career planning center, and the course unfolded in three stages: (a) exploring career and self, (b) exploring the selected occupation in relation to self, and (c) creating an action plan for meeting individual career goals and objectives. Course activities included various assessments and reflective writing; alumni roundtables; a short-term externship; and an e-portfolio, which served as an assignment and assessment tool for instructors. As students progressed through the integrated experience and grew in their understanding of self and career options, they were encouraged to modify, change, or further their intended major and goals. Campuses seeking to proactively address the struggles many sophomores face in terms of informed decisions and commitment to major might consider partnering faculty with career services professionals and adopting an integrated sophomore-experience course that is well-aligned with their specific campus population.

Steele, G. E., Kennedy, G. J., & Gordon, V. N. (1993). The retention of major changers: A longitudinal study. ***Journal of College Student Development, 34*****(1), 58-58-62.**

This study investigated the success of an Academic Alternatives program (ALT) developed for students considered at risk for dropping out due to indecision after a high number of credits and/or nonadmission to an intended and desired major within the university. While students were not referred to the ALT program based on class year, the referral criteria indicated that these students were likely sophomores and juniors. The program included group counseling workshops, career development resources and counseling, and a three-credit hour course designed to present academic alternatives and career-related information. There were 206 students in the ALT group and 206 in the control group. Multivariate analysis was conducted to determine the effect of the ALT program. Findings indicated those who participated in the program were more likely to feel confident about their major selection and persist until graduation. The results of this study suggested practitioners dealing with students in transition from one major to another or from undecided to a major should recognize the opportunity to help these transitioning students through more intentional generalist advising and career exploration assistance.

CHAPTER 2
The Transfer Transition

Similar to the growing population of transfer students at many colleges and universities, the body of scholarship on the transfer transition is increasing. This chapter, the most robust in the book, provides a review of much of the recent research, institutional initiatives, and book chapters describing the various programs, policies, demographics, and key issues with potential implications on the experience of the current transfer student population. Concepts associated with the uniqueness of the transfer transition, (e.g., cooling out, transfer shock, swirling, transfer gap choice, reverse transfer, vertical and lateral transfer) are introduced in this chapter.

Summary of Findings

The research annotated in this chapter demonstrates the nuances that exist in the transfer student experience, which will likely only intensify as more points of entry to and through higher education emerge. As the number of transfer students grows, with many students transferring multiple times during their undergraduate experience, some institutions have created programs and services to ease the transfer transition, but there is a need for additional work in this area. Research on transfer student orientation programs, learning communities, and seminars demonstrate that these intentional efforts can contribute to the academic confidence and success of transfer students. Furthermore, these programs can help transfer students begin to make connections with peers, faculty, and staff. Often, transfer students view these individuals as institutional experts who can help them navigate the process of adjusting to the culture of the new institution.

Despite programs aimed at fostering connections, developing trusted relationships can be a challenge for transfer students, especially when they transfer into institutions with larger class sizes and less in-class faculty interaction. While not always the case, it is often the students who transfer from two-year to four-year institutions who have the greatest difficulty making this adjustment. Without adequate support, these students may not feel as though they belong at their new institution, which places them at risk of not persisting.

For some students, perceptions of institutional bureaucracy, confusing organizational structures, and insufficient or inaccurate information become barriers to the transfer process. These barriers often negatively affect feelings of confidence and competence and may even lead to feelings of marginality. Academic advisors play an important role in the transfer process because they often offer information about the transfer of academic credits from one institution to another. Providing opportunities for students to easily access information about credit transfer through academic advisors, transfer centers, or online resources creates a pathway for the transfer process. As recent research has demonstrated, when transfer students are able to successfully make the transition, they can achieve the same or similar educational outcomes as their peers who are native to that institution.

Omissions and Areas of Future Research

While the volume of work referenced in this chapter might suggest there are few omissions or areas for future research, there is additional work to be done to better understand the transfer transition. For example, few empirical studies describe the potential impact of institutional initiatives on transfer student success, and there is also a need for published assessment or evaluation data related to these initiatives. Further, research comparing the experience of disaggregated populations of transfer students (e.g., lateral vs. vertical, sophomore-level vs. junior-level, traditional vs. nontraditional, minority vs. majority, low-SES vs. high-SES) would also add to the collective knowledge on the transfer transition.

Transfer Patterns

Beinke, J., Bond, D., Borocoman, Eklund, J., Goeman, J., & Lemoine, K. (2011). Transfer success and accountability: A Texas perspective. In M. A. Poisel & S. Joseph (Eds.), *Transfer students in higher education: Building foundations for policies, programs, and services that foster student success* (Monograph No. 54, pp. 101-112). Columbia, SC: University of South Carolina, National Resource Center for The First-Year Experience and Students in Transition.

This chapter described how the state of Texas has developed a system of statewide accountability to improve the transfer student experience. Through the implementation of the Closing the Gaps (CTG) plan, transfer data from colleges and universities in the state can be compared, leading to institutional improvements. Although the system promoted comparisons across institutions, not all types of institutions were held to the same measures of performance. For example, the authors mentioned the differences between performance indicators for two- and four-year institutions in Texas, including the point at which students transfer from community colleges, and the academic performance of students who have transferred from those colleges. This information is also captured in the Transfer Student Performance Report required by the state and providing data on vertical transfers. The authors demonstrated how these data could be used to track the flow of transfer students across institutions and found that, after six years, 40% of the full-time students at two-year institutions transferred across levels (i.e., two-year to four-year). In addition to examining transfer rates, the authors reviewed degree completion for transfer students and reported that the number of credit hours attempted in the first college year was related to graduation rates. Specifically, for transfer students who began at two-year institutions, only 12% who attempted fewer than 24 credit hours in the first year completed a bachelor's degree in six years. In addition to identifying transfer student patterns, the authors suggested other states collect and use similar types of student data to develop articulation agreements and other policies to improve the experience of transfer students.

Castañeda, C. (2002). Transfer rates among students from rural, suburban, and urban community colleges: What we know, don't know, and need to know. *Community College Journal of Research and Practice, 26*(5), 439-449.

The author of this article evaluated existing definitions of transfer students, transfer rates at rural and urban institutions, and demographic data for transfer students. From this information, she discovered there was no consistent definition of transfer, although she discussed the need to develop one. The author noted other issues concerning transfer students: (a) inconsistent methods of calculating transfer rates and (b) misconceptions of transfer students overall (i.e., increasing number of transfer students who continue to take courses at their original institution even after transferring). Adding to the complexity of the nature of student transfer are the inconsistent findings about transfer students from rural areas versus students transferring from urban areas. Existing data on minority transfer student retention suggested that these students struggle more than their majority peers who transfer, regardless of where (geographically) the students are transferring from and to (e.g., rural, urban). Finally, the author indicated that using state transfer data and data collected from national studies (e.g., National Transfer Assembly) can help create a more robust and accurate image of who transfer students are, what programs can and should be created to assist them, and how transfer programs and services could be evaluated.

De los Santos, A. G., & Wright, I. (1989). Community college and university student transfer. *Educational Record, 79*(3/4), 82-84.

The authors detailed the interinstitutional relationships that formed between Maricopa Community College District (MCCCD) and Arizona State University (ASU). This included MCCCD faculty serving on ASU curriculum committees, student services staff meetings to coordinate services and ease student transitions, and an academic consortium formed in 1983 to facilitate articulation and student transfer. Institutional data revealed that the percentage of ASU undergraduates who transferred from MCCCD increased during this period of collaboration, and a higher number of transfer students were found among upper-division enrollment. The data also showed increasing examples of reverse transfer (i.e., students transferring from ASU to a Maricopa community college) and swirling (i.e., moving among various institutions). Based on the findings, the authors recommended tracking systems be used to monitor student movements within higher education. They also wondered if similar nonlinear transfer patterns exist elsewhere and suggested comparable data analysis in other large urban areas.

Dowd, A. C., Cheslock, J., & Melguizo, T. (2008). Transfer access from community colleges and the distribution of elite higher education. *Journal of Higher Education, 79*(4), 1-31.

The authors of this article investigated the enrollment of low-income community college transfer students at elite institutions. Specifically, they examined the extent to which elite colleges and universities were enrolling transfer students, how many were from community colleges, and the socioeconomic background of those students. Using data collected from a national survey, they found that low-income students were overly represented at community colleges compared to elite institutions, although enrollment varied based on selectivity and the institutional type. For example, private selective institutions enrolled fewer transfers because of a preference for lateral transfers (i.e., from other four-year institutions). The majority of transfer students at all elite institutions were at the highest levels of socioeconomic status, but students from middle-income backgrounds had an increased chance of transferring to an elite institution if they were coming from a two-year institution compared to their peers transferring from a four-year institution. The authors indicated that overall preference for transfer students from four-year institutions was likely attributable to the level of academic preparation these students had compared to their peers from community colleges. Furthermore, elite institutions may have a reduced need to make up for lost enrollments because of low attrition rates. The authors also cited state articulation policies as another influence on the transfer student access to four-year institutions, including the elite colleges and universities in the study. They suggested future research on this topic examine student aspirations and choice, outreach and preparation programs (offered at two-year institutions), the relationship between degree attainment and cognitive and noncognitive variables, and transfer policies and procedures.

Li, D. (2010). They need help: Transfer students from four-year to four-year institutions. *The Review of Higher Education*, 33(2), 207-238.

This longitudinal study examined the degree attainment of students who transferred between four-year institutions. Attendance patterns, which the author identified as stayed, stop-out, interrupted transfer, and continuous transfer, were independent variables in the study. The findings indicated attendance patterns, age, gender, and race all had an impact on the graduation rates of participants in the study. Specifically, students who were not continuously enrolled were significantly less likely to graduate than students in the study who were continuously enrolled at a four-year institution. Further, students who transferred to another institution, but remained continuously enrolled at one institution or another, had a lower probability of graduating compared to students who remained at their home institution. Hispanic students were also less likely to earn a bachelor's degree, regardless of attendance patterns. The researcher indicated that social integration had a positive impact on participants' degree completion, but academic preparation and GPA in the first-year did not affect degree completion. The author suggested that transfer policies and incentives be implemented to encourage continuous enrollment.

Peter, K., & Forrest Cataldi, E. (2005). *The road less traveled: Students who enroll in multiple institutions* (NCES Report No. 2005157). Washington, DC: National Center for Education Statistics, U.S. Department of Education.
This report examined the phenomenon of multiple institution attendance, including transfer, co-enrollment, and attendance at a two-year college. The researchers examined enrollment histories and demographic characteristics for two groups: (a) a cohort of students who began postsecondary education in 1995-1996 and (b) students who attained bachelors' degrees in 1999-2000, regardless of when they began secondary education. They also administered surveys to determine the reasons why students enrolled in other institutions. One of the most salient findings was attending more than one institution was common among undergraduates. Additionally, community college students were more likely to transfer than those who began in four-year institutions. Among the students who began college in 1995-1996, those who attended three or more institutions were less likely to attain a degree. Multiple institution attendance also negatively impacted time to degree for the 1999-2000 degree recipients.

Wasser, R., Moore, C., & Shulock, N. (2004). Effect of racial/ethnic composition on transfer rates in community colleges: Implications for policy and practice. *Research in Higher Education, 45*(6), 651-672.
This study examined factors associated with community college transfer rates. Regression models were developed using community college data; the researchers particularly were interested in race or ethnicity as a variable. The analyses used two different definitions of the transfer rate. The more inclusive definition was calculated by dividing the number of transfers by the total number of first-time, first-year students in a given cohort for a period of three years. The more narrow definition, which was measured over six years, was calculated by dividing the number of students in a cohort who transferred by the number of students in the cohort who completed at least 12-credit hours and enrolled in transfer-level math or English. Although other factors expected to influence differences in transfer rates were held constant, the results revealed disparities in transfer rates by race and ethnicity, especially for Latino and African American students who demonstrated lower six-year transfer rates in colleges with higher percentages of these populations. The findings were consistent with those from previous studies: specifically, higher transfer rates were found in community colleges with a greater focus on academic programs and with student populations that were younger, of higher socioeconomic status, and with better academic preparation.

Factors Affecting Transfer Students' Adjustment and Success

Cabrera, A. F., Burkum, K. R., & La Nasa, S. M. (2005). Pathways to a four-year degree: Determinants of transfer and degree completion among socioeconomically disadvantaged students. In A. Seidman (Ed.), *College student retention: A formula for student success* (pp. 155-209). Westport, CT: Praeger.

Using data from the National Center for Education Statistics (NCES), this chapter explored the propensity of students from lower socioeconomic backgrounds (SES) to pursue higher education compared to their higher SES peers. The authors indicated that students in the lowest SES levels are likely to pursue higher education through two-year institutions but have very low bachelor degree completion rates compared to four-year institution peers. This was attributed, in part, to the low number of students who begin at two-year institutions and ultimately transfer to four-year institutions, as well as the degree aspirations, academic preparedness, and the quality of peer and faculty interactions. The authors found that high school academic preparedness and the courses taken at two-year colleges (specifically, math and science) had the greatest impact on transferability of low-SES students from two- to four-year institutions. To help this population, the authors recommended that students take math, science, and remedial reading (if necessary); become engaged with their peers, faculty, and staff; and receive encouragement (from family and peers) and financial aid. Changes were also suggested in institutional policies that focused on the responsibility of two-year institutions for transfer rates, especially since not all students enter these institutions with the desire to transfer.

Crisp, G., & Nora, A. (2010). Hispanic student success: Factors influencing the persistence and transfer decisions of Latino community college students enrolled in developmental education. *Research in Higher Education, 51*(2), 175-194.

The authors sought to discover what factors led to success in the second and third years of college for Hispanic community college transfer students, as well as the variables that impacted success among developmental and nondevelopmental students. Drawing from a wide range of institutional and federal data sources and student interviews, the researchers studied 570 Hispanic students who were enrolled at a community college (2003-2004) and intended to transfer to a four-year institution. The results revealed that success in the second and third years of college was positively influenced by enrolling in higher level math courses in high school, having parents with higher levels of education, and receiving more financial aid. Working more hours, being enrolled part-time, and taking developmental courses decreased the odds of success within the second and third years, with these findings being consistent with other studies. Number of hours worked, financial aid, and enrollment intensity influenced the success of both nondevelopmental and developmental students in the second year and nondevelopmental students in their third year but did not show a significant influence on developmental students in their third year. Based on their findings, the researchers recommended additional financial support for Latino students entering higher education and the implementation of institutional policy related to developmental students.

Dennis, J. M., Calvillo, E., & Gonzalez, A. (2008). The role of psychosocial variables in understanding the achievement and retention of transfer students at an ethnically diverse urban university. *Journal of College Student Development*, 49(6), 535-550.

This study examined the ways in which academic self-efficacy, college commitment, personal or career motivation for attending college, and support of peers, combined with age and first-quarter GPA, affected varying profiles of transfer students. Participants included 1,130 (67% female) transfer students attending a four-year, public, Hispanic-serving, urban university in southern California. Transfer students were asked to complete an online survey of college attitudes in a required orientation course. Researchers identified five distinct student profile groups: (a) young achieving; (b) mature achieving; (c) low peer support; (d) young, low-achieving; and (e) low confidence or commitment. The results indicated the five groups differed significantly with regard to ethnic makeup and in subsequent trajectories of academic achievement and retention (e.g., GPA at the end of the first transfer year, enrollment in subsequent semesters). The young, low-achieving group, who were primarily minority students (consistent with other research findings), appeared to be most at risk, with lower GPAs and graduation rates. The authors suggested that higher education administrators who work directly with transfers can benefit from obtaining information on the psychosocial characteristics of their students to help them access the services they need most.

Ehrenberg, R., & Smith, C. L. (2004). Analyzing the success of student transitions from 2- to 4-year institutions within a state. *Economics of Education Review*, 23(1), 11-38.

This article described a methodology, using data provided by the Office of Institutional Research and Analysis of the State University of New York, that can be used within state systems of higher education to evaluate how well two-year institutions are preparing students for a successful completion of a four-year degree. Further, the methodology can be used to assess how well the four-year institutions are educating and graduating those student who transfer from two-year institutions.

The authors suggested that administrators and policy makers examine those institutions at both ends of the spectrum (i.e., those that successfully prepare and graduate students and those that do not) to discover the factors that lead to higher performances on these measure.

Flaga, C. T. (2006). The process of transition for community college transfer students. *Community College Journal of Research and Practice, 30*(1), 3-19.
The purpose of this research was to gain a better understanding of the community college transfer student's transition to the four-year university. Using a qualitative research design with two data collection points, 35 community college transfer students were interviewed about their first semester at Michigan State University (MSU). A few months later, 30 of the students returned to share their experiences of their second semester. Two questions were asked: What is the nature of transition for community college transfer students during their first semester at a large, four-year university? and How do transfer students' experiences change between their first and second semester at the four-year university? The data led to the development of the five dimensions of transition: (a) learning resources, (b) connecting, (c) gaining familiarity, (d) negotiating, and (e) integrating. These dimensions were then assessed within the academic, social, and physical environments. Findings suggested the need to develop communication between advising at the community college and MSU; create transition programs, including orientation and transfer student seminars; and establish more opportunities for transfer student engagement and involvement on campus through mentor programs and living-learning opportunities. The implications suggested that community colleges and four-year institutions need to take necessary steps to facilitate transition, and students must also take the initiative to manage their own transition process.

Glass, J. C., & Harrington, J. (2002). Academic performance of community college transfer students and "native" students at a large state university. *Community College Journal of Research and Practice, 26,* 415-430.
This study compared the academic performance (GPA), degree of transfer shock, and retention and graduation rates for community college transfer students and native students at a Southern research institution. The sample consisted of 100 community college students and 100 native students within the College of Arts and Sciences. Data were collected from the Registrar's Office to compare GPAs at the end of students' lower-division work (i.e., end of sophomore year for natives and second year of community college for transfers) and at the end of their first and second semesters within their major coursework. The researchers found that transfer students had equal or better performance than native students at

the end of their lower-division coursework (sophomore year). Transfer students experienced transfer shock (decline in GPA) after their first semester in their major area of study but recovered after the next semester. Retention rates declined over time for both groups. The results suggested that institutions should be willing to admit community college students with qualifying GPAs but need to be ready with appropriate support services (e.g., counseling, tutoring, mentoring) to help prevent transfer shock.

Hagedorn, L., Cypers, S., & Lester, J. (2008). Looking in the review mirror: Factors affecting transfer for urban community college students. *Community College Journal of Research and Practice*, 32(9), 643-664.

This paper examined the factors that helped and hindered successful transfer from a two- to a four-year institution using a retrospective analysis. The data were collected as a part of the Transfer and Retention of Urban Community College Students (TRUCCS) Project, a five-year longitudinal initiative that examined data from 5,000 community college students across the nine campuses of the Los Angeles community college system. Surveys, phone calls, and National Loan Clearinghouse data were used to obtain knowledge about how many students had or had not transferred. Student transcripts were analyzed to ascertain grades, course completion, course-taking patterns, transfer readiness, and other indicators of success. The data revealed that the most predictive indicator of transfer was the successful completion of courses within the transfer-focused curriculum, including transfer-level English and math courses. The researchers recommended intrusive academic advising enmeshed within the classroom experience, where students are advised about the transfer-ready curriculum and encouraged to move through the sequences, including any developmental coursework, in a swift and continuous manner. Advising may be supplemented with interactive web-based systems, though these cannot serve as a proxy for in-person advisement.

Jacobs, B. C. (2004). Today's transfer students: Trends and challenges. In B. C. Jacobs (Ed.), *The college transfer student in America: The forgotten student* (pp. 1-14). Washington, DC: The American Association of Collegiate Registrars and Admissions Officers.

This chapter discussed the various transfer patterns in institutions all over the nation. It provided a brief historical perspective on these patterns and presented data and statistics about transfer students and trends gathered from the National Center for Education Statistics (NCES) and academic literature. Significant increases in the numbers of students attending community colleges with the goal of transferring to a four-year school were noted and attributed to multiple factors, including affordability, growing college-age populations, greater numbers of poor and ethnic students, and tougher admissions policies at some four-year institutions. The patterns of reverse, lateral, and multiple institution transfer were also discussed. The chapter described some of the difficulties faced by transitioning students and emphasized the need for both increased institutional support services and increased research on the topic of transfer students. The author noted that with the expansion of distance education, further information about the transfer and transition process for students moving among online, two-year, and four-year academic programs will be needed. This chapter may serve as an overview resource to those desiring to assess ways to improve transfer student transition and success. In addition, the gaps highlighted in the existing literature surrounding transfer students offer ideas for future research.

Jacobs, B. C., Busby, R., & Leath, R. (1992). Assessing the needs of transfer students. *The College Student Affairs Journal, 12*(1), 91-98.

In this study, traditional-aged transfer students from two different public intuitions ($N = 619$) participated in a quantitative needs assessment to determine which types of orientation programming might be most effective for this population. Students reported needing between "some" and "a lot" of assistance with academic advising or guidance depending on the campus, but most desired options over a directive approach. Findings also revealed that characteristics and needs of transfer students (a) are not necessarily the same as those of first-year students and (b) can vary across institutions, suggesting that assessment of the particular transfer population on each campus is needed if appropriate orientation programming is to be designed.

Kirk-Kuwaye, C., & Kirk-Kuwaye, M. (2007). A study of engagement patterns of lateral and vertical transfer students during their first semester at a public research university. *Journal of The First-Year Experience & Students in Transition, 19*(2), 9-27.

This qualitative study investigated the engagement of eight vertical transfer (VT) students (i.e., two-year to four-year institutional transfer) and nine lateral transfer (LT) students (i.e., four-year to four-year institutional transfer). The researchers used questions from the National Survey of Student Engagement (NSSE) to inform the interview protocol. The findings indicated that LT students were slightly less engaged than their VT peers, except in the area of student-faculty interaction, and both groups had lower levels of engagement than nontransfer peers. The researchers had hypothesized that LT students would be more engaged because they would be less likely to experience transfer shock since they had prior experience with a four-year institution; however, there was little difference between the two groups.

Differences in personal experiences of the LT students in the study (e.g., class size, faculty accessibility, perceptions of institutional support) appeared to influence their feelings of engagement at their new institution. VT students who had positive interactions with faculty at their two-year institution appeared to be more prepared and willing to be engaged with faculty at their new institution while those who had lower levels engagement in an active and collaborative learning environment were more likely to report feeling transfer shock. The participants from both groups who did not take part in new student orientation had poor supportive campus environments (academic and cocurricular) experiences. Based on the findings in the study, the researchers suggested that understanding and taking into consideration student background is an important aspect of planning and delivering orientation and transition programs for transfer students.

Laanan, F. S. (2001). Transfer student adjustment. In F. S. Lannan (Ed.), *Transfer students: Trends and issues* (New Directions for Community Colleges, No. 114, pp. 5-13). Hoboken, NJ: John Wiley & Sons.

In this chapter of a larger volume devoted to transfer students, the author discussed studies describing the behavior of students transferring from community colleges to four-year institutions, including data about the degree attainment of students transferring after earning an academic credential. These studies focused on how transfer students adjust, as well as the interaction of personal and demographic characteristics and institutional characteristics on that process. The author's analysis found that transfer students' GPAs following their transfer to a new institution tended to decline immediately after transferring but improved during subsequent semesters at the transfer institution, and native students outperformed transfer students in overall GPAs and persistence. Finally, the author drew from existing research to discuss the role of psychological approaches, educational environment, and campus climate on the retention and performance of transfer students.

Laanan, F. S. (2007). Studying transfer students: Part II: Dimensions of transfer students' adjustment. *Community College Journal of Research and Practice, 31*(1), 37-59.

This research sought to provide a better understanding of the complexities and frameworks present in the transfer and adjustment process from a community college to a four-year institution. The Laanan-Transfer Students' Questionnaire (L-TSQ) was completed by 717 students who had transferred from 64 different California community colleges. The L-TSQ measures noncognitive attributes in three areas: (a) social demographics, (b) community college experiences, and (c) four-year university experiences. Student responses were evaluated using descriptive statistics, exploratory factor analysis, and linear multiple regression. Findings indicated that demographic variables did not ultimately affect adjustment. Low intellectual self-concept or a low university GPA had a negative effect on student adjustment. Further data analysis pointed to the positive impact of social involvement and the quality (vs. quantity) of student effort. Those working to improve the transfer and transition process for students might use this information when designing workshops intended to increase student academic self-concept, prepare students for transition and transfer to the four-year institution, improve the effectiveness of study habits, or inform students of opportunities to socially engage on campus.

Laanan, F. S., Starobin, S. S., & Eggleston, L. E. (2010). Adjustment of community college students at a four-year university: Role and relevance of transfer student capital for student retention. *Journal of College Student Retention, 12*(2), 175-209.

This exploratory study examined the transfer experiences of students entering four-year institutions from two-year colleges. Of particular interest was the impact of transfer capital, which investigates the experiences and acquisition of knowledge needed to successfully navigate the transition process. Data were collected in 2004 and 2007 from 918 students via the Laanan-Transfer Students' Questionnaire. Respondents were overwhelmingly traditional-age and White, with nearly equal representation between the genders. Two hypothetical models were used to investigate the predictability of multiple factors on transfer adjustment. A significant finding was that students who learn positive study habits and skills at the community college have an easier time adjusting academically at the four-year institution. Student experiences with faculty at the four-year institution had the potential to be highly influential in a student's adjustment to the new institution. The authors noted that practitioners might use this information to provide students critical transfer success information during orientation sessions. The authors further suggested using this study as a launching pad to address transfer student needs and as a tool to inform future research on this population.

Lee, W. Y. (2001). Toward a more perfect union: Reflecting on trends and issues for enhancing the academic performance of minority transfer students. In F. S. Laanan (Ed.), *Transfer students: Trends and issues* (New Directions for Community Colleges No. 114, pp. 39-44). Hoboken, NJ: John Wiley & Sons.

This study used qualitative methods to explore the transfer experiences of minority students. The researcher conducted semistructured, focus group and one-on-one interviews with 12 African American students at a large, Research I university in the southeastern United States. Four themes that had a direct positive or negative effect on the success of transfer students in the study were identified: (a) policy, (b) programs, (c) performance assessment, and (d) people. For example, academic policy information shared with students before they transferred was outdated. Study participants appeared to rely on advice from their peers. As a result, these students may have received inaccurate policy and program information. The researcher suggested that institutions take a more active role to ensure minority transfer students receive accurate information through mentors or other faculty or staff. Students' overreliance on peers may have stemmed from what some described as uncomfortable interactions with faculty and staff of different races. They explained that this might have been attributable to differences in cross-cultural communication and suggested that faculty and staff receive training to help them be aware of nuances in communication with diverse students.

Long, B. T., & Kurlaender, M. (2009). Do community colleges provide a viable pathway to a baccalaureate degree? *Educational Evaluation and Policy Analysis, 31*(1), 30-53.

The authors compared the outcomes of community college students who transferred into public, four-year institutions in Ohio to those of similar students who initially enrolled in a public, four-year institution. After conducting an analysis of a detailed data set, the researchers tracked outcomes for nine years and used multiple strategies to deal with selection issues, such as student preferences, financial constraints, academic profiles, beliefs about the prospects of benefiting from the respective institutions, and other characteristics. Even when controlling for these variables, students who initially began at community colleges were significantly less likely (14.5%) to complete bachelor's degrees within nine years when compared to their peers who started at four-year institutions. This disappointing finding may, in fact, be conservative because the researchers limited their sample to students who had taken the American College Testing (ACT) placement exam; the authors admitted this had the potential to exclude from the study community college students who wanted baccalaureate degrees but failed to prepare for admission to four-year universities by taking the ACT. The study provided evidence for public and institutional policy makers to consider as they explore ways to boost the success of community college students who transfer to four-year institutions.

McIntosh, E. J., & Nelson, D. D. (2012). Transfer students: Thriving in a new institution. In L. A. Schreiner, M. C. Louis, & D. D. Nelson (Eds.), *Thriving in transitions: A research-based approach to college student success* (pp. 137-166) Columbia, SC: University of South Carolina, National Resource Center for The First-Year Experience and Students in Transition.

This chapter described the findings from the Thriving Quotient research study that involved 5,339 participants from 27 colleges and universities, including 614 transfer students. Data collected from transfer students indicated the most significant predictor of transfer success was student-faculty interaction. Engagement in campus activities, which might contribute to the students' perceptions of being part of the larger campus community, was also a strong predictor of transfer student thriving compared to native or nontransfer students in the study. While the transfer students overall thriving scores were consistent with native students, the social connectedness scores were significantly lower. In addition to not feeling engaged with the campus, transfer students' social connections in the study were also influenced by their dissatisfaction with the institution and perceptions about the lack of value of their tuition. The authors suggested these findings were likely associated with the logistical (i.e., transfer of credit hours earned at previous institutions), social (i.e., making connections with peers), and academic challenges (i.e., longer time to degree completion) transfer students experienced. To combat these challenges, the authors described successful programs at the University of Michigan, Vassar College, and the University of North Texas that were designed to enhance social connections, ease academic transitions, and increase the likelihood of thriving among transfer students.

Melguizo, T., Kienzl, G. S., & Alfonso, M. (2011). Comparing the educational attainment of community college transfer students and four-year college rising juniors using propensity score matching methods. *The Journal of Higher Education, 82*(3), 265-291.

This study used propensity score matching (PSM) estimates to investigate educational outcomes of 640 students who had transferred from two-year institutions compared to 2,520 third-year (junior) students who had completed two years at a four-year institution. When the researchers controlled for remedial credits, they found that both groups of students earned equivalent numbers of credits. Although there were no significant differences in credit hours earned, the researchers noted only a small number of participants from the community colleges actually transferred to a four-year institution although the majority expected to, with this finding being consistent with national studies. The researchers indicated that unclear transfer articulation policies, remedial course work, and financial needs affect students' ability to transfer from two- to four-year institutions.

Owens, K. R. (2010). Community college transfer students' adjustment to a four-year institution: A qualitative analysis. *Journal of The First-Year Experience & Students in Transition, 22*(1), 87-127.

In this article, the author described a qualitative study involving 57 students who were transferring from a community college to a four-year institution after earning 60 or more credit hours. The participants submitted e-journals, which were analyzed and coded for recurring themes and ideas to determine the perceptions of the success of their transfer and the supports and barriers to that process. Data collection began while the participants were still enrolled at the community college and continued through the midterm of their first semester at the four-year institution. Findings indicated that, while enrolled at their community college, students' perceptions of success focused on belonging and feeling comfortable at the four-year institution, and they felt entitled to more guidance from the four-year institution. These results were further confirmed as the researcher examined the supports students perceived as important to the success of their transfer, including personal attention and social and academic integration. Participants suggested changes they felt would enhance the transfer process, including implementing transfer orientation programs, creating checklists for transfer students, and developing a transfer advising program. The researcher indicated that while participants communicated a consumer-oriented view of the transfer process, suggesting that the institution would look after them, this mindset changed as students adapted to their new environment and became more comfortable.

Perez, P. A., & Ceja, M. (2009). Building a Latino/a student transfer culture: Best practices and outcomes in transfer to universities. *Journal of Hispanic Higher Education, 9*(1), 6-21.

This article provided a demographic overview of Latino/a transfer students, as well as student attendance, persistence, and transfer rates for this population. The authors indicated that most college-going Latino/a students begin at two-year institutions, and the literature also showed that these students are not likely to transfer to four-year institutions. Critical race theory (CRT) and validation theory were used to identify successful practices and programs that facilitate the transfer process for Latino/a students, such as more Latino/a role models and mentors among high school, community college, and university faculty and staff; streamlined articulation agreements; and culturally responsive outreach programs at all institutional levels. To build a transfer culture among this population, it was recommended that universities address any student development needs, make students more aware of dual access (or enrollment) programs, and encourage transfers to attend university orientation or enroll in student success courses. Finally, the authors suggested ways that would help universities to institutionalize structural interventions to help maximize transfer student success.

Peska, S. (2011). One size does not fit all: Tailoring orientation services to mid-year transfer students. *The Journal of College Orientation and Transition, 18*(2), 33-44.

This article highlighted research data produced from two studies on adjustment issues faced by transfer students who enroll midyear. The first study was conducted in 1999, using focus group interviews with 25 community college transfers seven weeks after their transition to a large, mid-Atlantic university. Ten years later, the author carried out a mixed-method study consisting of an online survey ($n = 353$) and focus group interviews ($n = 22$). Both studies revealed that community college transfer students experience adjustment challenges specific to the semester in which they transferred. They expressed difficulty building social relationships, managing personal adjustments, and becoming involved in extracurricular activities. In addition, the studies concluded that orientation services for midyear transfer students were lacking and that programming was needed to address this special population. The author suggested orientation professionals design opportunities for students to connect, create marketing materials specific to midyear transfer students, highlight on-campus employment opportunities, and prepare students for the differences they will experience in the classroom.

Smith, C. T., & Miller, A. (2009). *Bridging the gaps to success: Promising practices for promoting transfer among low-income and first-generation students. An in-depth study of six exemplary community colleges in Texas.* Washington, DC: Pell Institute for the Study of Opportunity in Higher Education.

The purpose of this study was to identify the promising practices for transferring students from two-year to four-year institutions. It examined the institutional characteristics, practices, and policies that might contribute to successful transfer. One part of the study consisted of a series of linear regression analyses to find successful community colleges in Texas. Six institutions met the success criteria for higher than expected transfer and graduation rates given their institutional and student characteristics, including first-generation status, SES, and English proficiency. The second part of the research consisted of a qualitative study of the six highest performing schools. The researchers conducted site visits and interviewed students, program directors, faculty, and administrators. Three common themes were found across these institutions: (a) structured academic pathways, (b) a student-centered culture, and (c) culturally sensitive leadership. A number of practices and strategies were suggested, including creating collaborative campus programs, engaging faculty in the transfer admissions process and performance, and establishing a culture of accountability.

Swigart, T. E. (2000). Learning and personal growth in community college students who intend to transfer: The role of student involvement, institutional environment, and advising. *Journal of Applied Research in the Community College, 8*(1), 43-55.

This study investigated the factors that contributed to personal growth among community college students who plan to transfer to a four-year university. It also examined the relationship between student effort and growth. Participants included a national sample of community college students (N = 7,734) who intended to transfer. Respondents were sampled from a national Community College Student Experiences Questionnaire (CCSEQ); data were collected from September 1999 through June 2000. The author found that students benefitted from talking with advisors and counselors about issues concerning their upcoming transfer to the university. It was recommended that community colleges offer transfer-student services with an emphasis on advising. Further, advisors and counselors should identify the particular needs of women and students of color.

Texas Higher Education Coordinating Board. (2011). *The Community College Transfer Student Report.* Retrieved from the Texas Higher Education Coordinating Board website: http://www.thecb.state.tx.us/

This report contained institutional profiles of public four-year institutions in Texas in an attempt to compare transfer student services and policies across the state. First, the Texas Higher Education Coordinating Board surveyed every public institution in the state, asking for a description of existing transfer pathways, articulation agreements, student outreach, and the like. The second part of the study compared native (i.e., those who initially enrolled at a university and had achieved junior status as of fall 2006 at that same university) and transfer students (i.e., those community college students who transferred into a university as juniors during the fall 2006 semester) at each institution. Data included application and admission rates, financial aid awarded, time-to-degree rates, and baccalaureate completion rates. Across all institutions, on average, transfer students completed college at a lower rate, took a longer time to graduate, and completed slightly more credits than their peers. Despite this disparity, the study also found that Texas public universities do make efforts to recruit, retain, and graduate transfer students; however, some institutions are more successful than others. It was recommended that universities share best practices across the state and that the faculty and administrators collaborate with transfer service providers at the community colleges on university advising.

Townsend, B. K., & Wilson, K. B. (2006). A handhold for a little bit: Factors facilitating the success of community college transfer students to a large research university. *Journal of College Student Development, 47*(4), 439-456.

The researchers in this study interviewed 19 students who transferred from a community college to a four-year, research-intensive university to investigate perceptions of the factors that affected the academic and social integration of these students. Participants discussed the support they received from the institution to which they were transferring; however, the majority indicated they had received no support or assistance from their community college. Although students expressed perceptions of support, they indicated that limited interaction with faculty at the four-year institution made them feel a lack of academic integration. Similarly, the participants discussed challenges in the area of social integration, specifically as they attempted to get to know their peers. The majority mentioned that it was easier to meet peers at the community college because of classroom size, existing social networks (e.g., attending the same high school), and similar characteristics (e.g., commuters, working while going to school). The researchers concluded that the most significant challenges for the study participants were associated with fitting in or feeling a sense of belonging at the new institution rather than concerns with the transfer-credit process. They suggested that because participants were used to a classroom environment that provided opportunities for social and academic engagement, the transition to the university classroom culture was challenging. Further, understanding the differences in the missions and structures of the community college and university environments is useful to help students understand what to expect when they transfer.

Wang, X., & Wharton, B. I. (2010). The differential patterns of college involvement between transfer and native students. *Journal of The First-Year Experience & Students in Transition, 22*(2), 49-66.

This research compared patterns of academic and social involvement for transfer and native students. The participants included 3,166 second- and third-year students (2,477 natives and 689 transfers) at a public, Midwestern, research institution. The students completed a 149-item survey including questions on student involvement in various campus academic and social activities, participation in student organizations, usage of student affairs services and university resources, satisfaction with the college experience, and demographic information. The results did not reveal significant differences between the two groups in terms of academic involvement. However, transfer students were less involved socially, participated less in campus events and student organizations, and used fewer support services. The results suggested that college educators (e.g., admissions and orientation professionals) should create policies and programs that encourage social involvement among transfer students and provide them with greater awareness of academic and social support services.

Wawrzynski, M. R., & Sedlacek, W. E. (2003). Race and gender differences in the transfer student experience. *Journal of College Student Development, 44*(4), 489-501.

This study examined the expectations, self-perceptions, past academic behaviors, and attitudes of transfer students at a mid-Atlantic, doctoral-extensive, public university. Participants were 2,492 incoming transfer students (53% female, 14% African American, 14% Asian American or Pacific Islander, 6% Hispanic/Latino/a, and 65% White, with a mean age of 21.8). During their university orientation, students completed the Transfer Student Survey (TSS). Multivariate statistical analysis revealed that not all transfer students share the same experiences and expectations when enrolling at a new institution. Race and gender impacted student expectations, behaviors, and outcomes. For example, women and students of color had a stronger desire for a sense of community; Hispanic students were more concerned with developing strong communication skills; and African American and Asian students exhibited the greatest interest in learning about other cultures. Students of color also expected to ease their transition and become part of the new university community by interacting with faculty and other students outside of the classroom. To better facilitate transfer students' transitions to a new environment, the researchers argued that administrators and those responsible for orienting transfer students to the university must be made aware of the specific experiences and expectations of transfer students.

Wolf-Wendel, L., Twombly, S., Morphew, C., & Sopcich, J. (2004). From the barrio to the bucolic: The student transfer experience from HSIs to Smith College. *Community College Journal of Research and Practice, 28*(3), 213-231.

This study examined the unique relationship between two urban, Hispanic-serving, community colleges and an elite private college, Smith College. To date, there has been little research on students who transfer to private schools. The authors interviewed administrators and current students at all three institutions and found the community college students who took advantage of the transfer agreement were diverse, but not necessarily by race or ethnicity. For instance, these students were likely to be returning adults or first generation. Once students enrolled at Smith, they experienced a mild form of culture shock and often noted there were major differences between the home cities and Smith's location in rural Massachusetts. After initial discomfort, most interviewees felt at ease on their new campus and did not experience major problems with transfer credits.

Barriers to Transfer Success

Alexander, B. C., Garcia, V., Gonzalez, L., Grimes, G., & O'Brien, D. (2007). Barriers in the transfer process for Hispanic and Hispanic immigrant students. *Journal of Hispanic Higher Education, 6*(2), 174-184.

The authors used ethnographic methods to explore the transfer barriers experienced by Hispanic students in the Dallas County Community College district, which tends to transfer Hispanic students at low or flat levels compared to White students. The researchers employed classroom observations of students enrolled in a cultural studies course along with face-to-face interviews of selected students and their key family members. The data were coded, and barriers were identified that hindered successful transfer to a four-year institution: (a) students' and their families' lack of knowledge of the higher education system; (b) lack of preparedness for college-level coursework; (c) limited or no English skills; (d) enrollment in nonacademic, nontransferable coursework; (e) limited financial resources; (f) cultural barriers to fitting in with a predominantly White student body; (g) students' failure to see the value and relevance of higher education; (h) lack of individual attention from faculty or staff; (i) cultural norms, especially for women, that do not support higher education; and (j) lack of financial aid for undocumented students. The authors concluded that more outreach to Hispanic students was necessary to overcome these transfer barriers. This included providing information (in Spanish) about the value of education, admissions requirements, and financial aid to both students and their family members; more one-on-one meetings with advisors and faculty members; courses that provide student-faculty mentoring relationships; and a transfer center or transfer staff who can address holistic student needs and help translate complicated articulation policies.

Bahr, P. (2008). Cooling out in the community college: What is the effect of academic advising on students' chances of success? *Research in Higher Education, 49*(8), 704-732.

The author explored Burton Clark's controversial proposition of cooling out—the idea that academic counselors dissuade underprepared community college students from pursuing their professed academic goal in lieu of one that is less ambitious. Clark placed specific emphasis on the role the academic counselor played in the cooling out process, and this study explored that role by examining the interaction between advisors and remedial math students, transfer-seeking students, and students of different races. The sample comprised 190,177 students enrolled in the California community college system in fall 1995 and drew from institutional data (e.g., transcripts, demographics, financial aid awards, degree and certificate awards). Bahr did not find evidence of cooling out; rather, he found that academic advising was effective in promoting success, particularly for those students who were underprepared. For future areas of research, he recommended exploring how different dimensions of advising (e.g., delivery, types, format, organization, timing) impact students' degree attainment.

Bensimon, E. M., & Dowd, A. (2009). Dimensions of the transfer choice gap: Experiences of Latina and Latino students who navigated transfer pathways. *Harvard Educational Review, 79*(4), 632-659.

This study focused on the transfer choice gap among Latino/a students—when students are academically eligible to transfer to a selective institution but instead choose to transfer to a less competitive institution or not transfer at all. As part of a larger study, the researchers interviewed five Latino/a students (three men, two women) who started their college education at a California community college to examine their pretransfer experiences. Among the sample, only one student transferred to a selective institution, despite the fact that four students were eligible. Each case study revealed different dimensions of transfer choice gap, the challenges and barriers these students faced, and the institutional factors that can influence transfer choices. The strongest finding was the absence of expert institutional transfer agents to provide information and guidance to students in a structured way. The authors noted that students in underrepresented groups may not feel entitled to ask questions and seek individualized counseling and support, or feel they belong at a selective institution, making intrusive outreach to these groups all the more important. Articulation agreements, web-based transfer information systems, and transfer policies were felt to be in vain without specially trained transfer agents to provide advocacy and role modeling to help students overcome informational and cultural barriers.

Bensimon, E. M., Dowd, A. C., Alford, H., & Trapp, F. (2007). *Missing 87: A study of the "transfer gap" and "choice gap."* (Long Beach City College and the Center for Urban Education, University of Southern California Report). Retrieved from http://cue.usc.edu/assests/CUE_Bensimon_Missing_87.pdf

This report described the findings of a comprehensive study of the transfer process at Long Beach City College (LBCC). The investigators, an evidence team composed of faculty, staff, and administrators, reviewed statistical and interview information to learn why some students eligible to transfer to selective universities chose not to. The team explored both transfer gap (i.e., comparison of the number of students eligible to transfer to a public California four-year institution to those who actually transferred) and choice gap (i.e., difference between LBCC students eligible to transfer to a selective university and those who actually did). During a three-year period following 27,422 LBCC students, 520 successfully completed the requirements to transfer to a four-year institution. This low number was attributed in part to the lack of transfer readiness, which the researchers felt should be developed as part of the mission of two-year institutions. Of the 520 students, 87 originally fell into the transfer gap category (later corrected to 112). When analyzed for race, the transfer and choice data indicated that African Americans and Hispanic/Latino/a students had transferred at greater rates than their peers. The investigators identified five areas with potential impact on transfer and choice gap: (a) informational, (b) structural, (c) practices, (d) policy, and (e) cultural. The report described the five areas in detail as well as barriers (e.g., limited interaction with counselors, high number of transfer credits accumulated, inadequate computer skills, transfer anxiety) and enablers (e.g., in-class transfer process presentations, improved transfer center signage, college visits, early intervention workshops). Potential solutions for each area were also offered.

Hagedorn, L. S., Moon, H. S., Cypers, S., Maxwell, W. E., and Lester, J. (2006). Transfer between community colleges and four-year colleges: The all-American game. *Community College Journal of Research and Practice, 30*(3), 223-242.

Using data from the Transfer and Retention of Urban Community College Students (TRUCCS) Project, a longitudinal study that examined data from 5,000 community college students across the nine campuses of the Los Angeles Community College District, the authors introduced a new way to conceptualize community college student progress toward transfer readiness and bachelor's degree attainment and identified factors that predicted success and barriers. The researchers pulled a subset of students who expressed the intention to transfer (n = 3,318) and analyzed their transcripts within the framework of California's transfer readiness curriculum. They sought to discover which curricular modules students were reaching, and which were the most challenging and distant; if there was a relationship between specific student demographics and academic progress; and any other factors that separated those who were or were not progressing. The results revealed that approximately half of the students had successfully passed any of the curricular modules, and only 3-4% attained transfer readiness. The authors asserted this might be due to the number of remedial classes that many community college students need to take, which lengthens the amount of time to reach transfer readiness. Indeed, those who became transfer ready typically did so within an average of nine and a half semesters, making the term two-year college a misnomer. The language requirement was the least likely to be completed.

Differences by ethnicity, gender, age, and native language were present, although modest. The authors stressed the importance of academic counselors in guiding students through their academic program and helping them to interpret policies.

Ornelas, A., & Solórzano, D. G. (2004). Transfer conditions of Latina/o community college students: A single institution case study. *Community College Journal of Research and Practice, 28*(3), 233-248.
This case study considered the barriers to transfer for Latino/a students at a community college in California. While Latino/a students composed about 70% of the 20,000 students enrolled in the college in fall 2000, only 667 students transferred to a four-year college or university. Study data came from surveys, focus groups, and personal interviews conducted with Latino/a students, counselors, faculty members, and administrators. Findings indicated that, while all groups found academic underpreparation and outside responsibilities to be an issue with the potential to negatively impact student transition and success in community college, the groups disagreed about many other barriers. Although only one of six administrators identified the transfer figures as problematic and something needing improvement, faculty and counselors noted the need for more institutional commitment and a stronger transfer culture. The authors found evidence of cultural deficit thinking on the part of administrators and counselors, which could also account for blame shifting and a lack of institutional commitment to improvement. Recommendations covering a wide range of topics—from learning communities to financial aid processes to pedagogy and technology—were offered to community colleges desiring strong transition supports and transfer programs.

Tobolowsky, B. F., & Cox, B. E. (2012). Rationalizing neglect: An institutional response to transfer students. *Journal of Higher Education, 83*(3), 389-410.
This study focused on an in-depth examination at an intentionally unnamed university using data collected from interviews conducted in 2005-2006 with 17 institutional agents (i.e., faculty and staff members with the potential to affect the transfer experience). Several common themes were found. For example, respondents commented on the students' diverse backgrounds and varying levels of academic credit, which made it difficult for the university to have a one-size-fits-all approach. Many noted institutional policies that prevented them from doing more for this population. Further, these institutional agents had limited awareness of transfer student concerns, such as social integration and lack of information about campus traditions. The authors suggested that rather than simply identifying characteristics among students, future studies should focus on the institutional contexts into which students are transferring.

Zamani, E. M. (2001). Institutional responses to barriers to the transfer process. In F. S. Lannan (Ed.), *Transfer students: Trends and issues* (New Directions for Community Colleges, No. 114, pp. 15-24). Hoboken, NJ: John Wiley & Sons.

Multidirectional student movement between two- and four-year institutions calls for a range of innovative transfer services. This essay provided an overview of the barriers facing students, particularly low-income, non-Asian students of color, who plan to transfer from a community college to a four-year institution. These challenges included financial background and academic readiness as well as institutional factors, such as campus diversity. The author also emphasized the importance of well-defined articulation agreements between two- and four-year schools. Finally, the essay gave an overview of successful programs that facilitated the transfer process for community college students, such as campus transfer centers, clear articulation and admission agreements, outreach activities, information sessions, campus tours, and improved skills acquisition programming. Los Rios Community College, Glendale Community College, and Santa Ana College were highlighted. In terms of future policy changes, the author noted that senior institutions could use the transfer process to recruit and admit diverse students.

Institutional Initiatives

Anderson, R. D., & Sundre, D. L. (2005, September/October). Assessment partnership: A model for collaboration between two-year and four-year institutions. *Assessment Update, 17*(5), 8-16

The authors discussed three ways in which Blue Ridge Community College (BRCC) and James Madison University (JMU) have collaborated in their assessment efforts related to students who have transferred from BRCC to JMU. The first area of collaboration involved assessing learning outcomes, which included measuring student learning related to technology and information literacy skills. The second area related to sharing software, resulting in the creation of three shared assessments between the two institutions. Finally, the third area concerned graduate students collaborating with BRCC to develop materials for an assessment workshop and related assessment activities. Although the article did not quantify any assessment findings related to the aforementioned collaborative efforts, the authors discussed how these collaborations had helped advance the overall impact of assessment at both institutions. For example, the authors described how the articulation agreement between the institutions can be assessed using the student learning outcomes data. Further, because many students do transfer from BRCC to JMU, both institutions can use the shared assessment data to know more about the knowledge and skills of their students and make adjustments to academic programs and articulation agreement.

Austin, S. (2006/2007). A successful university-foundation partnership to assist transfer women. *Journal of College Student Retention, 8*(3), 275-296.

This qualitative report examined a comprehensive university academic support program for nontraditional, female, transfer, commuter students to determine its success in promoting academic and social integration. The public, Northeastern institution received a grant through the Avon Foundation as a means of supporting women in higher education. Nine women were selected for two years of partial scholarship aid, based on their GPA, academic recommendations, and financial need. The average age of the participants was 35, and all but one woman had children. Seven of the nine participants were interviewed using a semistructured questionnaire to explore their experiences with the program and its impact on their success as a student. Program administrators and faculty mentors were also interviewed and/or surveyed. At the completion of the study, among the seven women interviewed, five had graduated and two were completing their degrees. The data suggested that financial aid, academic counseling, orientation, mentoring, and peer support meetings helped the women transition from a small community college to a large university. To ensure the success of nontraditional populations, the author recommended that educators consider the following: (a) the fiscal and symbolic support of scholarships; (b) programs that offer peer connectedness; (c) early exposure to academic resources; and (d) individual help based on academic, personal, and family issues.

Eggleston, L. E., & Laanan, F. S. (2001). Making the transition to the senior institution. In F. S. Lannan (Ed.), *Transfer students: Trends and issues* (New Directions for Community Colleges, No. 114, pp. 87-97). Hoboken, NJ: John Wiley & Sons.

This chapter reviewed literature related to transfer student support programs. The first section detailed the characteristics of transfer students and described their needs once they reached senior institutions. The authors asserted that issues related to admissions, registration, orientation, cultural diversity, negative perceptions, academic advising, course articulation, and financial concerns need to be addressed to help students successfully earn a bachelor's degree. Despite the fact that a large number of four-year institutions do not have specific transfer student programs, some model initiatives do exist. The authors described the Exploring Transfer (ET) program at Vassar College, the Transfer Summer Program (TSP) at UCLA, the Office for Non-Traditional Students at the University of Arkansas, and the Multicultural Transfer Admissions Program at the University of Illinois at Urbana-Champaign. Among the four programs described, only ET and TSP showed success in promoting higher retention and graduation rates for transfer students. The authors concluded there is a need for further research that focuses on program development and evaluation of support programs for transfer students, along with policy implementations that will promote the success of these students.

Hagedorn, L. S., Cabrera, A., & Prather, G. (2010). The community college transfer calculator: Identifying the course-taking patterns that predict transfer. *Journal of College Student Retention, 12*(1), 105-130.

This article described a software application called The Community College Transfer Calculator, a tool designed for the Los Angeles Community College District, which can be adapted for other colleges, districts, and states. The calculator was created to ascertain the key indicators of transfer for community college students, how the completion of certain courses and grades impacts transfer, what factors can be derived from transcript data, and how this can be transformed into a user-friendly tool. Such data can be useful to different audiences, including academic advisors, instructors, institutional researchers, and policy makers. The authors described the design and methodology behind the calculator and discussed seven potential scenarios in which the tool would be useful.

Hagedorn, L. S., Lester, J., Garcia, H., McLain, M., & May, A. (2004, November). *Transfer center stories: A mission, a plan, or missed opportunities?* (Transfer and Retention of Urban Community College Students [TRUCCS] Project Report). Los Angeles, CA: TRUCCS.

The authors examined the role of transfer centers at the nine community colleges within the Los Angeles Community College District to understand the role they play in promoting the successful transfer of students to senior institutions. A case study approach was employed, which included interviews with the transfer center directors, student focus groups, and written observations of the centers. The themes that emerged from the student focus groups included knowledge (e.g., lacking knowledge about the transfer process and available resources), academics (e.g., being academically underprepared, resulting in frustration with time to degree completion), and finances (e.g., being uninformed about financial aid resources and needing to work while going to school). The two main themes identified through the interviews with the center directors included institutional support and external influences. Institutional support focused on the center location (centrally located vs. out of the way); staff that was transient and part-time; lack of outreach programming (e.g., Transfer Days); and the need for money for resources, such as new equipment, field trips, and seminars. External influences included the student population, who were often underprepared and required a high level of support. One external influence that proved to be extremely effective in supporting the student transfer process was ASSIST, a website that helped students navigate the transfer process within the California public system. The authors concluded that transfer centers need greater support and will be most effective when they are centrally located with an appropriate number of academic advisors to provide individualized and intrusive support for students.

Handel, S. J. (2011). *Improving student transfer from community colleges to four-year institutions: The perspective of leaders from baccalaureate-granting institutions*. New York, NY: College Board.

This seven-part report focused on institutional practices that support successful community college transfer. Data collected were qualitative, coming from interviews with 21 leaders at 12 four-year institutions of varying size and selectivity. Documented in the report are programs and practices that were designed to create a successful transition both into community and four-year colleges. Some programs included advisors from the four-year campus having office space at the community college, transfer student housing on campus, summer bridge programs, dual enrollment (in both two- and four-year institutions), transfer orientation sessions, strong assessment and data collection practices, specialized courses for transfer students, and peer mentor programs. For the smoothest transitions, faculty at two-year institutions and administrators at four-year institutions should collaborate often about ways to improve transfer student success. Those committed to recruiting more transfer students or creating more effective transitions programs into or from the community college setting will find best practices in the report that can be evaluated for adoption or adaptation at another institution. This piece can also serve as a guide for institutional self-assessment about the practices, attitudes, and culture of a campus for transfer student transition and success.

Hoffman, A. J., & Wallach, J. (2005). Effects of mentoring on community college students in transition to university. *Community College Enterprise, 11*(1), 67-78.

This study investigated whether a mentoring program could assist underrepresented community college students in building confidence toward a future transition to a four-year institution. The specific mentoring program used group work and outdoor gardening with 27 community college student participants and 10 mentors attending a four-year university. Community college students worked with their mentors in the community college garden, met faculty members at the four-year institution, and toured the local four-year campus with their mentor. Findings indicated this type of cooperative program raised the self-esteem and academic commitment of the participants and contributed to positive feelings for mentors as well. While addressing attrition and transition for all students is valuable, community college campuses with high populations of minority students and/or high attrition and low transfer rates to four-year institutions might investigate other collaborative mentoring programs.

Hoover, S. C. (2010). Designing orientation and transition programs for transfer students. In J. Ward-Roof (Ed.), *Designing successful transitions: A guide for orienting students to college* (Monograph No. 13, 3rd ed., pp. 181-192). Columbia, SC: University of South Carolina, National Resource Center for The First-Year Experience and Students in Transition.

This chapter described the transfer student process and presented several programs and supports institutions have in place to assist this population. A discussion of existing literature presented challenges faced by the transfer student. A review of institutional websites and personal communication with various administrators at multiple institutions provided a snapshot of institutional initiatives to support the success of these students The author argued institutions should consider the specific characteristics of their transfer students and determine students' needs before planning programs to support this population. Significantly, empirical research on the success of these initiatives appears to be almost nonexistent. Assessment, evaluation, and publication of data on such programs would inform the profession on how to best help transfer students.

Lord, V. B., Coston, C. T. M., Davis, B., & Johannes, K. S. (2012). The impact of a discipline-based learning community on transfer students: A multi-dimensional pilot study. *Journal of The First-Year Experience & Students in Transition, 24*(2), 63-84.

This study used qualitative and quantitative methods to determine the longitudinal effect of participation in a yearlong, discipline-specific transfer student learning community. The Criminal Justice Learning Community (CJLC) was created to assist incoming community college transfer students with their transition to a research university and their academic major. A majority of the students in the CJLC were juniors and just over half were traditional-aged. Through two learning community seminars (fall and spring), students in the CJLC were exposed to the criminal justice major as well as myriad campus resources. In addition to the seminars, CJLC students received academic advising. Researchers determined that CJLC students (a) showed increased levels of involvement and engagement in the university, the criminal justice major, and related campus activities; (b) developed strong connections to CJLC faculty and peers, which helped overcome feelings of stress associated with transfer; and (c) demonstrated increases in academic success, measured by GPAs and survey responses related to study-habit variables.

Marling, J. L., & Jacobs, B. C. (2011). Establishing pathways for transfer student success through orientation. In M. A. Poisel & S. Joseph (Eds.), *Transfer students in higher education: Building foundations for policies, programs, and services that foster student success* (Monograph No. 54, pp. 71-87). Columbia, SC: University of South Carolina, National Resource Center for The First-Year Experience and Students in Transition.

The chapter created a case for orientation programming for transfer students by shedding light on the models, approaches, roles of faculty and staff, framework, and assessment essential in implementing a program that addresses their unique needs. The authors contend transfer students are not considered in the development of orientation programs, often resulting in a bland duplication of first-year orientation for these students. They suggested that providing a variety of quality programs will confirm the student's decision to enroll at the institution as it builds flexibility and displays commitment to the individual and his or her life circumstances. Facilitating a mandatory orientation program is a win-win situation because expectations can be consistently communicated. It requires a collaborative approach from student affairs and academic affairs departments, thus ensuring a consistent message and presenting a cohesive vision for orientation. In addition, the authors suggested that to develop an orientation program reflective of the transfer student population, orientation professionals must know the developmental and demographic profiles, create an appropriate framework shaping students' expectations, provide timely and effective communication, use current transfer students as peer mentors, incorporate student-faculty interaction, and implement self-assessment and program evaluation.

Mayhew, M. J., Vanderlinden, K., & Kim, E. K. (2010). A multi-level assessment of the impact of orientation programs on student learning. *Research in Higher Education, 51*(4), 320-345.

This study drew from data collected in a national survey of 14,208 transfer and first-year students at 35 institutions to assess the influence of orientation participation on student learning. Specifically, the investigators examined the role of four institutional variables: (a) institutional control, (b) undergraduate enrollment, (c) sponsoring division, and (d) whether or not the institution had a dedicated orientation office. The findings revealed that transfer students in the study were more likely to attribute personal gains in academic skills (e.g., time management and study strategies) and in their overall understanding of academic expectations to participation in orientation programs. Conversely, the researchers found that transfer students reported that orientation did not help them make social connections. With respect to the four institutional variables, the researchers indicated there were few significant findings. The only finding that appeared to have a slight impact on some of the participants was the existence of a dedicated orientation office.

Robertson, H., Trapani, S., & Hopkins, E. (2011). Advising and orienting transfer students: A two-pronged approach to improving transitions. *Journal for College Orientation and Transition, 19*(1), 103-111.

The article highlighted changes made to new transfer student orientation at Stony Brook University, a large, suburban state institution in the Northeast. In addition to redesigning transfer student orientation, a new-student seminar for transfers was implemented. Before 2008, transfer student orientation evaluations were poor, revealing that students' time was not well used. Transfer students also requested assistance beyond that of an orientation leader. A pilot program was launched using 30 academic advisors to assist with transfer student advisement. Students had the opportunity to register for a transfer-specific, first-year seminar, and over a four-year period, enrollment in this seminar increased from 74 to 1,000 students. The authors concluded that large, research universities could have success implementing more personalized orientation programs and new student seminars for transfer students. Investing in transfer students' initial transition could increase their chance of success.

Policies Supporting Transfer Success

Boswell, K. (2004). Bridges or barriers? Public policy and the community college transfer function. *Change, 36*(6), 22-29.

This article advocated for the community college as a vital institution for providing postsecondary access and, ultimately, upward mobility. Two-year colleges are especially important for students of color, who tend to lag behind their White counterparts in educational participation and attainment. Citing data from a longitudinal study by Adelman on two- to four-year institution transfer rates and recommendations from a national Access to the Baccalaureate Roundtable, the author built the case for what community colleges offer and how coursework transferability is of critical importance to the entire higher education community. The article explored this issue through the lens of access, transfer function, transfer policy barriers, and state and system policies. A brief list of resources was offered as well as 13 specific recommendations from the Roundtable intended to help policy makers promote smooth transitions through the educational system toward the attainment of a bachelor's degree.

Cohen, A. M.(2005). The future of transfer. ***Journal of Applied Research in the Community College, 12*****(2), 85-91.**

This article explored the student transfer process from two-year to four-year institutions from three perspectives. First, the author defined transfer rates as "the number of students matriculating at a community college in a given year and who complete ten or twelve units there, divided into the number of that group who enroll within a specified time, usually four to six years" (p. 86) and discussed how they are calculated. The second perspective concerned institutional and state policies, which can affect transfer rates. The author pointed out ways that institutions can make changes to policy and structure to encourage the ease of transfer for students. For example, creating common course numbering systems, accepting part-time students into evening courses or programs, allowing students to transfer more course work, and agreeing on a common understanding of transfer rates could all contribute to improvements in the transfer process. Florida was presented as a model of a state that has invested in community college programs to encourage students to begin their academic careers at these institutions. Lastly, Cohen explored why transfer rates differ among institutions and why some have rates above or below the average for their state. He noted that transfer rates are influenced by institutional characteristics, programs, location, and student demographics. In conclusion, the author felt transfer rates will continue to increase in the future and that community colleges will need to ensure that processes are in place for all students who wish to take their education to the next level.

de la Torre, D. (2007). Where there's a web, there's a way: Statewide approaches to promoting community college student transfer. ***Journal of College Admission, 194*****, 6-11.**

This article discussed how web-based transfer and articulation systems, which state higher education systems increasingly are making available to students, can facilitate the transfer process from two- to four-year institutions. Such systems can help to clarify and make widely available transfer policy information, present transfer articulation pathways, and offer comprehensive course equivalency database systems. They might include information about private baccalaureate institutions in statewide transfer agreements and identify campus-based contacts to personalize the process. States with notable web-based systems include Florida, Minnesota, New Jersey, North Carolina, and Wisconsin. For example, some offer comprehensive resources about college admission, academic degree requirements, financial aid, career information, childcare resources, disabilities supports, and credits for prior learning. Minnesota also provides information from neighboring states, including course equivalencies and campus contacts. North Carolina offers a transcript manager, allowing students to submit high school transcripts electronically along with their college applications. The author cited such systems as exemplary transfer practices worthy of further development given the increasing numbers of community college students who need to navigate these educational systems.

Furbeck, L. E. (2011). Enrollment management for transfer students. In M. A. Poisel & S. Joseph (Eds.), *Transfer students in higher education: Building foundations for policies, programs, and services that foster student success* (Monograph No. 54., pp. 13-28). Columbia, SC: University of South Carolina, National Resource Center for The First-Year Experience and Students in Transition.

This chapter described existing research and best practices involving enrollment management practices aimed at transfer student populations. The growing numbers of transfer students, particularly those transferring from two-year to four-year institutions, coupled with the increasingly diverse needs of these students were two of the reasons cited for examining enrollment management practices. The author described transfer student demographic variables and explained that to maximize enrollment capacity institutions should examine the availability of upper-level courses and academic majors. He also discussed the significance of financial support for this population, which could play an important role in the recruitment of prospective transfer students. Transfer processes, including credit transfer and evaluation, can have an impact on the recruitment and eventual enrollment of transfer students. The author indicated that these processes are often perceived as barriers, leading to situations where students transfer back to their home institution because their credits have not transferred as expected, or they end up swirling (i.e., moving from one institution to another). Recommendations included (a) the development of transfer orientation programs at four-year institutions allowing transfers to register with their native peers who have accumulated the same number of credits and (b) explicit and early communication with prospective transfer students at two-year institutions to develop stronger relationships with the college and clarify the transfer of credits. Finally, the author advocated for the development of structures that will allow a seamless transfer process, including creating a common general education or core curriculum among institutions that are part of a system.

Hagedorn, L. S., & Lester, J. (2006). Hispanic community college students and the transfer game: Strikes, misses, and grand slam experiences. *Community College Journal of Research and Practice, 30*(10), 827–853.

This article reported select findings of The Transfer Game, a five-year longitudinal initiative of the Transfer and Retention of Urban Community College Students

(TRUCCS) Project, which examined data from 5,000 community college students across the nine campuses of the Los Angeles Community College District. From this overall sample, researchers analyzed the transcripts of 3,151 community college students who had expressed an intention to transfer and coded them within the framework of California's transfer readiness curriculum. Researchers focused on data for Hispanic students by gender, age, and native language. After an average of more than six semesters, less than one third of the Hispanic community college students had passed a single curricular module, and only 8.9% were transfer ready. Though Hispanic females tended to progress at slightly higher rates than males, there were no differences with regard to age or native language. The authors suggested several policy changes to strengthen the number of Hispanic students who attain transfer readiness. At the K-12 level, these included using only experienced, credentialed teachers; enacting programs to help more teachers become fully credentialed; and offering teacher accountability programs to ensure quality education. For community colleges, the authors stressed the need for highly trained academic counselors with realistic caseloads, allowing for adequate monitoring and outreach to students; tutoring programs; and innovative curricula that challenge students of differing developmental levels.

Helm, P. K., & Cohen, A. M. (2001). Leadership perspectives on preparing transfer students. In F. S. Lannan (Ed.), *Transfer students: Trends and issues* (New Directions for Community Colleges, No. 114, pp. 99-103). Hoboken, NJ: John Wiley & Sons.

This chapter discussed ways that community colleges can prepare students for the transition from community college to a four-year institution. The authors noted that practices such as internal assessment, consistent data collection, and research regarding the current state of transfer are essential to ensuring transfer success. Setting a transfer agenda, raising the expectation of transferring, and monitoring articulation agreements are key in preparing students for the transition from the community college to the four-year school. Strong transfer programs often have linkages to four-year institutions that help to promote a smooth transition. Administrators at institutions seeking to ensure a strong transfer program should evaluate the perception and reputation of transfer at their institution and be intentional about sending the message that a community college is a serious path to achieving a bachelor's degree.

Kisker, C. B. (2007). Creating and sustaining community college—University transfer partnerships. *Community College Review, 34*(4), 282-301.

This study used a lens of network embeddedness theory to examine the transfer partnership between nine community colleges and a four-year research institution. A qualitative case study approach using participant observation and interviews was employed to closely examine the social networks present in this partnership, which at the time of publication was in its fifth year. While there were six main findings in the study, this article focused on two: (a) the challenges with governance and managing of partnerships and (b) the important role faculty should play in the partnerships. Collaboration was often hindered by strong opinions and questions of ownership of how certain elements would practically play out on campuses. In spite of the challenges, all participants felt the partnership to be successful to some degree and essential in transitioning students from high school to community college and from community college to four-year institutions. Partnerships were identified as ways to increase transfer numbers, enhance student awareness of transition and transfer issues, and create a culture of transfer. Findings had implications for future research, including expanding partnerships to include high schools; providing stipends or release time for faculty committed to partnering and working on the issue; and involving faculty in the collaboration process, which should be mutually initiated.

Rhine, T., Milligan, D., & Nelson, L. (2000). Alleviating the transfer shock: Creating an environment for more successful transfer students. *Community College Journal of Research and Practice, 24*(6), 443-453.

This article discussed the transition issues facing community college students and outlined recommendations for educators to support their successful transfer to a four-year college and completion of a bachelor's degree. The authors described the environment of two-year versus four-year institutions and discussed the factors that can impede and enhance degree completion in both types of settings. They suggested that informational workshops, repeated contact with university referral sources, mentor-mentee programs, advisor connections, articulation agreements, financial incentives, and tracking systems can promote a smooth transfer to university life and enhance graduation rates.

Shaw, K. M., & London, H. B. (2001). Culture and ideology in keeping transfer commitment: Three community colleges. *Review of Higher Education, 25*(1), 91-114.

This in-depth comparative analysis explored how institutional culture and ideology are reflected in transfer policies and practices at three community colleges. The three case studies were urban institutions that had high transfer rates and also formal and informal practices promoting transfer culture. A team of ethnographers conducted formal and informal interviews with students, faculty, staff, and administrators; attended events; and collected historical and archival documents. From a content analysis of more than 2,000 data elements, a profile emerged of these institutions. It was found the cultural aspects of each college reflected their underlying ideologies. Thus, students must negotiate the specific culture of their institution in order to transfer successfully. It was argued that while the procedural aspects of the transfer process are important, future research and practices should take into consideration what transfer means to the student, his or her family and friends, and society as a whole.

Shugart, S. C., & Harrison, D. T. (2011). Partnerships and student pathways. In M. A. Poisel & S. Joseph (Eds.), *Transfer students in higher education: Building foundations for policies, programs, and services that foster student success* (Monograph 54, pp. 43-53). Columbia, SC: University of South Carolina, National Resource Center for The First-Year Experience and Students in Transition.

Part of a monograph that served as a comprehensive guide to understanding and addressing the needs of transfer students, this chapter provided a national and regional perspective on the various pathways transfer students take to earn a baccalaureate degree. The authors discussed the changing demographics of transfer students and the increasing admissions requirements and cost of enrolling in a four-year institution. To reach the goal of graduating more students with the baccalaureate degree, they argued institutions need to partner to develop policies and practices that create unique, educational pathways based on a student's life circumstances and personal goals. Further, the authors suggested administrators and policy makers consider programs, curricula, and support services and structures that would align and provide these pathways for transfer students. The chapter included a case study describing statewide efforts in Florida to (a) brand and market academic programs; (b) guarantee admission to colleges and university partners to students graduating from participating community colleges, and jointly advise students who plan to participate in this program; (c) expand facilities and programs; and (d) revise curricula and articulation agreements.

Townsend, B. K., (2001). Blurring the lines: Transforming terminal education to transfer education. In D. D. Bragg (Ed.), *The new vocationalism in community colleges* (New Directions for Community Colleges, No. 115, pp. 63-71). Hoboken, NJ: John Wiley & Sons.

The author provided a historical overview of terminal education in the community college system. A terminal degree seeker was defined as a community college student with an educational goal of immediate entry into the workplace rather than pursuit of a bachelor's degree. This track is in contrast to students who take general education courses at a community college in preparation to enroll at a four-year institution (i.e., transfer education). It is common to refer to terminal education as vocational programs, such as those in the health professions, business management, administrative services, and applied science. The author noted that although some institutions have historically classified academic programs as transfer versus nontransfer, students traverse between these categories. For example, there were more terminal degree students seeking to transfer to four-year colleges and universities. As such, university policy makers need to pay more attention to the articulation of nontransfer degrees. Further implications for practice included increasing transferable general education courses in terminal programs and requiring higher credentials for faculty teaching in applied programs.

Wellman, J. V. (2002). *State policy and community college-baccalaureate transfer.* Washington, DC: The National Center for Public Policy and Higher Education, and The Institute for Higher Education Policy.

This report examined the relationship between state postsecondary and transfer patterns among two- and four-year institutions. The six states in this study—Florida, New York, North Carolina, Arkansas, New Mexico, and Texas—all relied heavily upon transfer from two-year schools to provide access for low-income and underrepresented students. The author surveyed institutions and compared Integrated Post-Secondary Education System (IPEDS) data for first-time, first-year student enrollments in degree producing institutions in fall 1991 with baccalaureate degree recipients in 1996-97. The study found there was little difference between the high-performing (Florida, New York, and North Carolina) and low-performing (Arkansas, New Mexico, and Texas) states in their basic approaches to transfer policies. Rather, it appeared that states with a comprehensive, integrated approach to transfer policy performed better than those that focused primarily on transfer strictly as an academic and institutional matter. Among other things, the author recommended states develop policies that relate funding and accountability to academic strategies.

CHAPTER 3

The Senior Year and Transition Out of College

The last four decades have seen a concerted effort placed on examining the transition into college, but it has only been in the last 15 years that the senior year has begun to receive the same level of attention. Truly, the senior year and transition out of college are milestones in the lives of students, and the pathways to and through these experiences are often as diverse as the students themselves and the institutions they attend—suggesting a broad landscape for examination and study. However, in the years since the 1998 publication of *The Senior Year Experience* (Gardner, Van der Veer, & Associates), one of the first in-depth explorations of the senior-year transition, there has been very limited research on the outcomes of the programs those authors described or areas they identified needing further examination. This chapter presents the available literature and best practices aimed at seniors and their transition out of college.

While the end of the senior year is usually marked by a rite of passage (i.e., commencement exercise), this culminating event is often preceded by many programs designed to prepare students for the transition into (a) their last year, (b) the world of work and postcollege life, and/or (c) further education. The annotations listed herein are on research or descriptions of several of these efforts, such as senior seminars or capstone courses, the senior-year experience as a whole, career development initiatives, and postcollege adjustment preparation. In addition, the citations explore challenges, issues, and characteristics unique to senior students and recent graduates, as well as the commencement ritual itself.

Summary of Findings

The programs described in this section respond to the need to provide seniors with opportunities to become experts in their academic majors and in soft skills (i.e., written and verbal communication, analysis, and critical thinking). Recent research suggests the need to prepare seniors for the diverse, interconnected world they will experience in the workplace. Indeed, the majority of literature found on the transition out of college focused on career adjustment. Capstone courses and senior seminars can offer these opportunities and help students develop their postgraduate skills while considering more broadly about how to integrate the college experiences with other aspects of their thinking and learning. Students appear to benefit from these courses whether they are part of an academic major or general education.

A holistic approach to programming, implementation, and reflection was offered by researchers who examined the entire senior-year experience, exploring both institutional efforts and student needs and characteristics. Much like the other student transitions described in this book, the success of programs for seniors relies heavily on how well faculty and staff understand and respond to the unique needs of this population. The research and practices documented here underscore the need to develop programs and services that provide academic and social support for seniors.

Omissions and Areas of Future Research

Although there is a body of literature describing some of the efforts focused on the senior year and the transition out of college, there is an absence of empirical research on the outcomes associated with those programs. To truly understand the impact of senior initiatives, faculty and staff should extend the existing self-reported data through empirical research on these programs and the students who participate. Further, to provide a long-term perspective, efforts should be made to track graduated students and determine how their collegiate experiences affect their postbaccalaureate lives. Finally, more work needs to be done on how seniors, particularly women and underrepresented students, can be psychologically and emotionally prepared for the impending transition out of college.

Challenges and Pathways Through the Senior Year

Allen, J., & Taylor, K. (2006). The senior year transition: Women undergraduates search for a path. *Journal of College Student Development, 47*(6), 595-608.

This qualitative study of 20 senior-level students at a Midwestern, four-year liberal arts institution with a total enrollment of 1,400, focused on the pathways women take to get through college. The women, selected through purposeful sampling, were divided into two equal groups: (a) *pathmakers* (i.e., those who changed majors several times before settling on one) and (b) *searchers* (i.e., those who changed majors several times and had difficulty staying in their current major). The researchers expected to find significant differences between the groups, but their inductive analysis also revealed several similarities. Both groups felt their parents provided reassurance and support throughout their journeys; however, searchers tended to have more economic support than pathmakers. Contrasts included (a) emotional tone with which their journey was related, (b) resources and people consulted in planning, (c) sense of self and future goals, (d) processes surrounding the attainment of future plans, and (e) intentions surrounding their current and future families. The authors offered suggestions for institutions to support women in their pathmaking and/or searching during college, including providing concrete guidance and direction to students early in their careers, encouraging students to become more self-reflective and stronger critical thinkers, and offering out-of-class experiences (e.g., service-learning or internships in the early years of college). Finally, the authors indicated this research could further theoretical approaches to knowledge making.

Freeman, K. (1999). No services needed? The case for mentoring high-achieving African American students. *Peabody Journal of Education, 74*(2), 15-26.

This qualitative study investigated the perceived role and influence of mentors on college transition experiences of high-achieving African American students. Twenty-one students attending various public and private institutions of higher education (after having been named one of several Top High School Seniors by *Ebony* magazine in 1994 and 1995) were interviewed. Semistructured interviews took place annually for four years, and the students also completed a questionnaire each year. The data indicated that "Students found the relationships extremely important to their initial adjustment to their institution, in their stay there, and in their transition from their institution to graduate school or the work environment" (p. 20). Mentors included faculty, staff, and off-campus community members, and they supported students through challenging transitions, such as solidifying a major and deciding whether to attend graduate school. The transition out of college was particularly difficult, and mentors served important support roles during times when students were considering career and graduate school options. While mentors were essential during transition times for these high-achieving students, the mentoring structure was generally informal with students finding their own mentors. The author recommended that campus leaders might consider formalizing the mentor program, especially for this population of students, in order to ease various transitions (into college, during major selection and change, and during the transition out of college).

Henscheid, J. M. (2008). Institutional efforts to move seniors through and beyond college. In B. O. Barefoot (Ed.), *The first year and beyond: Rethinking the challenge of college transition* (New Directions in Higher Education, No. 144, pp. 79-87). Hoboken, NJ: John Wiley & Sons.

This chapter examined the entire senior-year experience, beginning with definitions and various components of what it means to be a senior. Five key institutional efforts to assist seniors were summarized: (a) senior seminar and capstone courses, (b) career preparation programs, (c) opportunities to make intellectual connections, (d) programs that celebrate senior-year achievement, and (e) programs that create cohesion among seniors and alumni. The author noted there is often not the same level of institutional collaboration for supporting the senior year as there is in supporting students within their first year. Further, there is frequently a disconnect between supporting students' intellectual and vocational needs. The importance of providing opportunities for seniors to synthesize and reflect upon liberal learning skills (e.g., critical thinking, writing, global knowledge), which will serve them well in an ever-changing work environment, was also stressed.

Hunt, P. F., Boyd, V. S., Gast, L. K., & Mitchell, A. (2012). Why some students leave college during their senior year. *Journal of College Student Development, 53*(5), 737-742.

The authors of this article addressed a little-studied group of students—those who leave college altogether during their final year of studies. Data were collected over a 10-semester period from a withdrawal survey administered to students officially leaving a mid-Atlantic, public, research university within two semesters of graduating ($N = 464$). There were significant differences among various minority groups. Specifically, African Americans and Hispanics were overrepresented in the sample. Broadly, however, 61% of those withdrawing indicated that they were receiving familial pressure to do so. Additionally, 60% stated they were working at least 28 hours a week, and first-generation students in particular indicated that financial concerns contributed to their need to withdraw. Other commonly listed reasons for withdrawing midsemester included grades they were anticipating (perceived to be low or failing), not feeling socially connected with the campus, and overall issues with their chosen majors. The authors suggested several avenues for mitigating these concerns, including creating units to work with families of college students so that they can better support the students while they are enrolled; ensuring that students have adequate access to mental health resources to deal with stress and burnout; and working to engage students, particularly non-White students, in activities that will increase their sense of belonging on campus. Additionally, they recommended more purposeful and intentional advising of students in their final semesters on campus, as well as offering workshops to students on the costs and benefits associated with working a high number of hours off campus. Finally, the researchers stated that by noting these concerns and potential solutions, academic advisors and student affairs professionals across campus could help alleviate students' need to withdraw just prior to actual graduation.

Hunter, M. S., Keup, J. R., Kinzie, J., & Maietta, H. (Eds.). (2012). *The senior year: Culminating experiences and transitions.* Columbia, SC: University of South Carolina, National Resource Center for The First-Year Experience & Students in Transition.

This book was organized into three sections: (a) Understanding College Seniors, (b) Addressing the Needs of College Seniors, and (c) Facilitating the Transition Out of College. The first section provided a comprehensive description of today's college seniors, an overview of student development theories that serve as a foundation to understand the transition through and out of college, and a discussion of the implications technology has had on the learning and development of these students. Section II delved into the values, benefits, institutional examples, and considerations for high-impact practices aimed at seniors. This section also described senior seminars and capstone courses and the goals for these curricular experiences. In the final section of the book, the authors explored the impending transition out of the senior year and the roles career development and academic advising play in that process. Senior rituals and rites of passage as well as the transition to alumni status were also examined. The book concluded with a summary of the best practices described in the previous chapters and a call for purposeful reflection and integration of efforts aimed at the success of seniors.

Kinzie, J., Thomas, A. D., Palmer, M. M., Umback, P. D., & Kuh, G. D. (2007). Women students at coeducational and women's colleges: How do their experiences compare? *Journal of College Student Development, 48*(2), 145-165.

The purpose of this study was to compare the engagement experiences of students from different backgrounds at coeducational and women's colleges. The study sample consisted of 42,112 female first-year and senior undergraduates who completed the National Survey of Student Engagement (NSSE) in 2000, 2001, and 2002. Among the participants, 4,676 hailed from 26 women's colleges, and the remainder attended 264 coeducational institutions from the same Carnegie classifications. The results revealed students attending women's colleges engaged in educationally purposeful activities at higher levels than their counterparts at coeducational institutions. This may be attributed to the greater number of interactions between female students and faculty outside of class, which in many instances resulted in those faculty members becoming mentors to the students. The researchers indicated those relationships could assist participants as they consider career options and graduate study. Additionally, participants at women's colleges had greater gains in self-understanding, independent learning, and the ability to work effectively with others. The researchers concluded that female faculty and staff mentors, along with greater opportunities for engagement both in and out of the classroom, contributed to this finding. Students of color tended to be less engaged than White students. Transfer students were more than or equally as engaged as students who started and graduated at the same school. The findings suggested that women's colleges are transfer-friendly and may offer benefits that coeducational institutions do not provide them.

Louis, M. C., & Hulme, E. (2012). Thriving in the senior-year transition. In L. A. Schreiner, M. C. Louis, & D. D. Nelson (Eds.), *Thriving in transitions: A research-based approach to college student success* (pp. 167-190). Columbia, SC: University of South Carolina, National Resource Center for The First-Year Experience and Students in Transition.

This chapter described a qualitative research study of 22 senior-level Truman Scholars (a very competitive national scholarship program) from various colleges and universities, examining the experiences, behaviors, and attitudes that contributed to their student success. Three common qualities or themes were identified from the participant narratives: (a) curiosity, (b) drive, and (c) passion. Within the curiosity theme, students demonstrated a willingness to embrace uncertainty and, in instances of failure, learn from those experiences even if they made the students uncomfortable. Drive and passion were demonstrated by examples of self-awareness, personal motivation, and fervor that had an impact on decision making and sense of purpose. The researchers recommended strategies to instill the qualities of curiosity, drive, and passion within students, such as preparing them for the transition out of college as early as the first year, cultivating mindfulness and conscious risk taking, using appreciative advising as a catalyst to help them discover passions, and increasing opportunities that emphasize intrinsic motivation rather than extrinsic rewards.

Packard, B. W., Walsh, L., & Seidenberg, S. (2004). Will that be one mentor or two? A cross-sectional study of women's mentoring during college. *Mentoring and Tutoring, 12*(1), 71-85.

In this paper, the authors compared the nature of college women's mentoring experiences in their first and fourth years of their undergraduate studies. The participants included 261 college women (146 first-year students and 115 fourth-year students). The study contrasted the mentoring desired and experienced by first-year students who had recently left high school with seniors who would soon enter the workplace. Students indicated the structure of mentoring they would like to have and had actually experienced, using (a) agreement ratings on a Likert-type scale and (b) a forced-choice response. The authors found that first-year college students were more likely to desire mentoring in the form of one mentor, while seniors were more likely to desire more than one mentor. While both first-year students and seniors reported having a combination of family members and school-related adults who mentored them, college seniors were more likely to have college professors or academic advisors as mentors. The authors theorized that a one-size-fits-all approach to mentoring might not be appropriate during the college years. For example, seniors might need more help preparing for the workplace or graduate school, as opposed to transitioning to college. The authors further suggested that a networking model may be appropriate for college seniors as they seek employment and/or graduate school opportunities.

Taub, D. J., Servaty-Seib, H. L., & Cousins, C. (2006). On the brink of transition: The concerns of college seniors. *Journal of The First-Year Experience & Students in Transition, 18*(2), 111-132.

The authors of this research noted that much of the existing literature on the senior year was either theoretical in nature or dealt with only one aspect of the transition (e.g., career). The goals of this research study were to design a more useful, succinct version of the Senior Concern Survey (SCS) and use the new version to look at senior transitions through a multidimensional lens. Participants were 166 male and female students residing in residence halls. They were predominantly White

(73%) with a mean age of 22. The shortened SCS survey contained 31 items and had high internal consistency. Notable differences in the senior-year experiences were found depending on student characteristics (i.e., race, gender, and selection of major). For example, minority women reported concerns about career and graduate school discrimination, as well as lack of support from their family members. Further, students in majors associated with specific careers (i.e., agriculture, education, and engineering) all expressed less concern than those broader majors that are often associated with graduate school attendance (i.e., liberal arts, science, and management). Future research should investigate the interaction of multiple variables on the senior-year transition, especially with students from other campuses and those living off-campus.

College to Career Transition

Bowers, P. J., Dickman, M. M., & Fuqua, D. R. (2001). Psychosocial and career development related to employment of graduating seniors. *NASPA Journal, 38*(3), 326-347.

The authors of this article set out to examine the relationship among psychosocial development, the extent to which students participated in activities pertaining to their careers, and their ultimate employment status postgraduation. Just over 400 seniors who enrolled in one of 21 senior capstone classes at a medium-sized, land-grant institution in the Southwest completed the Student Developmental Task and Lifestyle Inventory (SDTLI). The SDTLI provides results related to three developmental tasks: (a) establishing and identifying purpose, (b) developing mature interpersonal relationships, and (c) gaining academic autonomy. In addition, participating students completed the Career Activities Survey (CAS), developed for this study, and provided researchers access to their final GPAs and employment status postgraduation. An analysis of the CAS yielded five factors (a) general job search activities, (b) career planning activities, (c) use of placement resources, (d) interactions with faculty, and (e) workshop attendance. Using multiple regression, the researchers compared the developmental tasks on the SDTLI with the survey factors and found there was a great deal of similarity between psychosocial development and career development, such as participation in career planning or job development activities, being associated with in higher levels of maturity. Additionally, the researchers noted a stronger relationship between employment status and involvement in career activities than between the former and psychosocial development, suggesting that the extent to which students are psychosocially developed may indicate their readiness to begin career-related activities.

Brown, S. C. (2004). Where this path may lead: Understanding career decision-making for postcollege life. *Journal of College Student Development, 45*(4), 375-390.

This research study sought to better understand the myriad elements that influence a college graduate's postcollege career path. The author used qualitative research methodology involving semistructured interviews with 18 women who graduated from a highly selective, women's liberal arts institution. Data analysis involved constant comparative naturalist inquiry. Results indicated this population made postcollege decisions based on the type of environments in which they found themselves, their orientations to learning (i.e., precollege experiences, attitude about college, personal traits that impact learning), their individual experiences (i.e., in- and out-of-class experiences that challenged them to consider other options and perspectives), and their interactions with influential individuals (i.e., parents, older friends, faculty, advisors, and staff). The author recommended intentionally addressing the often stressful and uneasy time of transition out of college through formal orientation to the postcollege decision-making process. Practitioners and researchers might use the author's model of postcollege decision making, including the elements of student experiences and self-reflection, student orientation to learning, interaction with others, and narrowing options to the point of a decision, as they plan or evaluate programs aimed at supporting the transition out of the institution.

Bulger, S. M., & Lindauer, J. R. (2007). Infusion of a professional development curricular strand across an undergraduate program. *Journal of The First-Year Experience & Students in Transition, 19*(2), 87-110.

This study focused on a curricular intervention designed to assist students in the preparation for the transition out of college. Faculty members in the human performance program collaborated with career services staff to develop and investigate the impact of using a three-course curricular strand to address professional development issues with undergraduate human performance students at a public, regional, Midwestern institution. Students enrolled in two different kinesiology courses ($N = 53$), generally taken during the sophomore to senior years, were invited to complete a survey and participate in one of two follow-up focus groups ($n = 18$). Findings indicated nearly all students appreciated the inclusion of postcollege, career information in the curriculum. Lessons learned by participating students included (a) understanding the importance of using career and academic advising services early in their college experience; (b) recognizing that preparing for postcollege careers should be taken responsibly, reflectively, and seriously; and (c) realizing the importance of networking and professional organizations to future career opportunities. Based on the findings of the study, the authors suggested practitioners and faculty working with students in a variety of majors consider how a curricular intervention in the early and midcollege years might ease the impact of the transition out of college.

Gardner, P., & Perry, A. L. (2012). Transitioning into the 21st century workplace: Will seniors be ready? In M. S. Hunter, J. R. Keup, J. Kinzie, & H. Maietta (Eds.), ***The senior year: Culminating experiences and transitions*** **(pp. 135-154). Columbia, SC: University of South Carolina, National Resource Center for The First-Year Experience & Students in Transition.**
The chapter opened with a description of the job market facing college graduates during the second decade of the 21st century. Gardner and Perry contend that a tightening job market is compounded by a skills gap for recent graduates along with attitudes and behaviors that are not congruent with workplace demands. The authors described a number of strategies to ameliorate these challenges and help students make a successful transition to the workforce, including internships, practica experiences, service-learning, and other experiential learning activities. Further, the authors suggested faculty and staff can support this transition by guiding students in their career explorations, introducing them to organizations and individuals connected to their career goals, inviting students to engage in reflection and move outside their comfort zone, and serving as student advocates. The chapter also included insights into the kinds of challenges students experience as they make the transition into the workforce, which may help career development specialists, faculty, and others develop and/or redesign initiatives designed to support seniors making this transition.

Hart Research Associates. (2010). ***Raising the bar: Employers' views on college learning in the wake of the economic downturn*** **(AAC&U Report). Retrieved from the American Association of Colleges and Universities (AAC&U) website: http://www.aacu.org/leap/public_opinion_research.cfm**
Commissioned by the Association of American Colleges and Universities (AAC&U), this report presented the findings from interviews with employers (N = 302) with at least 25% of their staff holding degrees from two- or four-year institutions. The results indicated that 75% of those interviewed did not think colleges and universities adequately prepared students for the workplace or global economy. The researchers suggested students needed a more liberal education providing them with cultural knowledge, critical-thinking and teamwork skills, civic responsibility experiences, analytical skills, and the ability to integrate and apply knowledge and skills to the working world, as well as more opportunities to

learn content associated with their major. The employers interviewed noted they were more likely to hire graduates from four-year institutions, particularly those with skills in the aforementioned areas. Further, the employers suggested communication, decision-making, and research skills, as well as the ability to create and innovate, were key areas of focus for institutions to better prepare students for the transition out of college.

Imbimbo, P. V., Nina, C. M., & Stein, E. A. (2005). The career development of college seniors. In P. A. Gore (Ed.), *Facilitating the career development of students in transition* (Monograph No. 43, pp. 177-194). Columbia, SC: University of South Carolina, National Resource Center for The First-Year Experience & Students in Transition.

The authors contend that the primary developmental task for college seniors is career planning rather than the career exploration that marks the early college years. They presented a case study of developmentally focused academic and nonacademic career services offered to upper-level students at Baruch College, part of the City University of New York. Academic career initiatives included communication-intensive courses designed to offer the skills students needed to compete for internships and full-time employment, a capstone course for business majors, a senior thesis requirement in programs where students routinely pursued graduate studies, and informal mentoring by faculty. Nonacademic career services and programs included individual career counseling, on-campus recruiting, an online career-management system, and other innovative uses of technology to support career planning and placement, career preparation workshops in interview skills and résumé writing, and a peer education program providing résumé review and interview preparation. Though focused on a single institution, the authors concluded the chapter with a series of recommendations applicable to a variety of institutional types and settings.

Hathaway R. S., Nagda B. A., & Gregerman S. R. (2002). The relationship of undergraduate research participation to graduate and professional education pursuit: An empirical study. *Journal of College Student Development, 43*(5), 614-631.

This study explored the impact of undergraduate research on students' transition out of college and into graduate school, particularly for students of color. The researchers surveyed alumni who participated in the University of Michigan's Undergraduate Research Opportunity Program (UROP) between 1989 and 1994 and compared their responses to those who applied to but were not admitted to the program. The sample included 183 alumni who had participated in undergraduate research and 108 alumni who had no undergraduate research experience. Just over 47% of the respondents were students of color. The study found that many non-UROP students had participated in some type of undergraduate research and that both UROP and non-UROP research had a positive impact on students. Further, these students were more likely to pursue graduate or professional school and to remain in contact with faculty than their peers. Another major finding was that undergraduate research benefits students of varying abilities, not just those who demonstrate high competence (e.g., honors students).

Hunter, A. B., Laursen, S., & Seymour, E. (2006). Becoming a scientist: The role of undergraduate research in students' cognitive, personal, and professional development. *Science Education, 91*, 36-74.

This qualitative study was conducted at four liberal arts colleges. The researchers interviewed students and faculty engaged in research during summer 2000. Interviews took place in summer 2000, before the students' spring 2001 graduation, and during 2003-2004 when students were alumni. While the student participants noted considerable positive aspects of the research experience, the authors focused on the faculty responses. Faculty indicated that as a result of the research experience, the students developed attitudes and behaviors that would help them continue as science researchers beyond their undergraduate careers. Faculty also observed the students took greater responsibility for their work and developed an increased interest in science. They saw these gains as evidence students were developing as young science professionals and believed these experiences would help with the transition to graduate school. The authors recommended similar studies at large research universities.

Magolda, P. (2003). Saying good-bye: An anthropological examination of a commencement ritual. *Journal of College Student Development, 44*(6), 779-796.

In this study, the researcher explored the constructs of a commencement ceremony at a medium-size, public university in the Midwest. He used three lenses to examine the ceremony: (a) the history and context of the exercise; (b) a view that "knowledge is partial, positioned, and incomplete" (p. 780); and (c) a perspective that interpretations are constructed within a social environment that can be influenced by the observer. An anthropological approach was used involving an analysis of comprehensive field notes taken before, during, and after the activity. The author compared the ceremony to a five-act play: (a) act 1, the welcome; (b) act 2, the awarding of an honor to a faculty member; (c) act 3, the delivery of inspirational advice from a prestigious keynote speaker; (d) act 4, the recognition of achievements and bestowing of student degrees; and (e) act 5, a call to action. The author's analysis offered the reader a comprehensive understanding of what is involved in the commencement exercise, as well as disconnects between the intent of the ceremony and the actual execution of various portions. Magolda suggested all campus rituals be examined in an effort to determine whether they accomplish their goals, are meaningful, and meet the intent and values of the institution, rather than just being events for the sake of the occasion.

Murphy, K. A., Blustein, D. L., Bohlig, A. J., & Platt, M. G. (2010). The college-to-career transition: An exploration of emerging adulthood. *Journal of Counseling & Development, 88,* 174-181.

Qualitative methodologies were used, including individual interviews, narrative analysis, and transcript coding, were used to better understand individual experiences and to allow for the emergence of common themes. Outcomes of the study revolved around five themes: (a) the importance of social support, (b) expectations and their impact on experiences, (c) optimism about the future, (d) postcollege adjustment, and (e) adjustment to the first job. The authors emphasized the impact and importance of social support during the transition from college to career and suggested that career counselors could play a pivotal role in offering services and programming to graduating seniors to better prepare them for workplace challenges. The student experiences documented in this article might influence the ways in which career counselors, those in transition programming, and faculty teaching senior seminars or capstone courses work with students preparing to enter the workforce.

Plunkett, M. (2001). Serendipity and agency in narratives of transition: Young adult women. In D. P. McAdams, R. Josselson, & A. Lieblich (Eds.), *Turns in the road: Narrative studies of lives in transition* (pp. 151-175). Washington, DC: American Psychological Association.

This research, a follow-up to an earlier study conducted by the same author, offered insight into how women transitioning from college to career make meaning of circumstances and develop a sense of professional identity. Using qualitative and quantitative methods, the author studied 24 of the original 40 college women five to six years after their graduation, with eight interviewed at greater depth. A narrative of one of the eight was presented in detail. Findings indicated that for the majority of participants, time out of school was used to solidify career choices and develop intimate relationships. Most women discussed the purposeful decisions they made as they contemplated career and educational opportunities; conversely, they also talked about the serendipity that occurred, leading them to jobs they would have never otherwise considered. Those working with women approaching their college graduation and transition out of the institution might use this research to more deeply understand the struggles and considerations of women in transition and better prepare themselves to assist these students on their path of solidifying their own career identity.

Wendlandt, N., & Rochlen, A. (2008). Addressing the college-to-work transition. *Journal of Career Development, 35*(2), 151-165.

This article reviewed the literature on the transition from college to the workplace to identify student challenges and develop a theoretical framework for appropriate institutional interventions. The authors highlighted three specific challenges: (a) changes in environmental culture, (b) graduate inadequacies in terms of experience or skills, and (c) inaccurate expectations of the transition from college to the world of work. Using a model of organizational socialization based on the work of several theorists, the authors discussed proposed stages of anticipation, adjustment, and achievement. Research suggested that career counselors have the opportunity to be more closely involved in the college-to-work transition for graduating students and that this model can provide a framework for considerations when working with this population. Beyond that, multiple practical suggestions for ways in which campus career professionals can intervene and assist this population were presented.

Yang, E., & Gysbers, N. C. (2007). Career transitions of college seniors. *Career Development Quarterly, 56*(2), 157-171.

In this study of 191 college seniors, the authors used canonical correlation analysis to better understand how students' self-efficacy and psychological distress aided or interfered with their psychological resources and focus on their career searches. Participants completed four different inventories: (a) the Career Search Efficacy Scale (CSES), (b) the Brief Symptom Inventory (BSI), (c) the Career Transition Inventory (CTI), and (d) the Behavioral Inhibition System and Behavioral Activation System (BIS/BAS). The results indicated that students who exhibited lower levels of career search self-efficacy and increased psychological distress tended to also have lower levels of psychological resources. Additionally, students with higher anxiety levels and efficacy related to personal exploration were shown to have increased readiness for the transition to a career. While the authors noted additional research is needed on the methods used in this study, the outcomes indicated helping students improve their own self-efficacy and decrease their psychological distress should result in easier career searches and, ultimately, transitions into careers over the course of time.

Yazedjian, A., Kielaszek, B. J., & Towes, M. L. (2010). Students' perceptions regarding their impending transition out of college. *Journal of The First-Year Experience & Students in Transition, 22*(2), 49-70.

The 183 senior students who participated in this research were invited from a larger pool of participants in a longitudinal study on college adjustment and achievement. The seniors completed a questionnaire concerning their thoughts and perceptions about the transition out of college, and content analysis of responses to open-ended survey questions was used to identify consistent themes and ideas. The findings indicated the majority of participants thought their undergraduate experience had prepared them for this transition to work, and they expressed a strong desire to apply what they had learned in coursework to their day-to-day work. Although confident in their preparation for this transition, students indicated they would draw on relationships with family and friends to help them through this experience; few stated they would use any institutional resources to help them during this period. For some, concern about the unknown (e.g., how long it would take to find a job or be admitted to graduate school) muted their excitement. The researchers found that, even with these concerns, students were reluctant to seek help from campus career centers or services.

Senior Seminars and Capstone Courses

Brooks, R., Benton-Kupper, J., & Slayton, D. (2004). Curricular aims: Assessment of a university capstone course. *The Journal of General Education, 53*(3), 275-287.

This article discussed a long-standing interdisciplinary capstone course at a liberal arts institution and the process and outcomes of the course assessment. A 46-item survey based specifically on the objectives of the curriculum was given to 168 students enrolled in the capstone course. Results indicated that students identified the capstone as assisting them to demonstrate leadership skills, clarify their personal sense of values and ethics, appreciate differences, improve oral and written communication skills, and gain awareness of social justice issues. Students also documented that the course did not play much of a role in improving critical-thinking skills.

Brownell, J. E., & Swaner, L. E. (2010). *Five high-impact practices: Research on learning outcomes, completion, and quality.* Washington, DC: Association of American Colleges & Universities.

Chapter 5 in this monograph described capstone courses and projects. The authors noted the lack of discussion about capstone courses over the past 10 years, which they attributed to the integration of many of these courses into the area of undergraduate research. Furthermore, they indicated the lack of a common definition and goals for capstone courses has also contributed to the absence of information about these curricular experiences. For example, some capstones are embedded in an academic major, providing a culminating learning experience connected to that area of study, while other courses are part of the general education, focusing on the transition out of college and into the working world. In the literature review, the most commonly cited goals for capstone courses were connected to a student's major. Finally, the authors found a lack of empirical research on capstone courses and projects, with existing research being limited in scope. The notable exception was the National Survey of Student Engagement (NSSE), which provided an annual snapshot of participation in capstone courses and the outcomes associated with those experiences. The authors concluded the chapter with the recommendation that goals and definitions for capstone courses be developed and used to guide assessment and further development of these programs.

Collier, P. J. (2000). The effects of completing a senior capstone course on student identity. *Sociology of Education*, 73(4), 285-299.

The author examined the process by which students identified with the role of *college student* by surveying students enrolled in senior capstone courses, as well as a group not enrolled in a course. A survey was developed for this study consisting of four scales: (a) critical thinking, (b) group skills, (c) social action and/or volunteerism, and (d) media resource skills. Students completed the measure in a pre- and posttest format, taking it twice each time: first for themselves and then as though they were comparing themselves to their peers. A composite score was calculated for each student allowing for regression analyses to be conducted between the two groups. In all cases, pretest scores predicted posttest scores. The analyses revealed that students who were enrolled in a capstone course more closely identified with the role of being a college student and that the course provided an excellent opportunity to apply their learning experiences to a nonacademic setting. The author concluded that universities should assess their students to determine if, in fact, they are impacting students in the manner they state: namely, that college helps students grow and prepare for life after graduation.

Padgett, R. D., & Kilgo, C. A. (2012). *2011 National Survey of Senior Capstone Experiences: Institutional-level data on the culminating experience* (Research Reports on College Transitions No. 3). Columbia, SC: University of South Carolina, National Resource Center for The First-Year Experience and Students in Transition.

This report included data from 268 colleges and universities that had at least one capstone experience at their institution. While the majority of reported capstones were discipline-based (59.6%), other types included a senior thesis or research paper, exhibition of the arts, internships, interdisciplinary courses, and comprehensive exams. Data were collected on the primary campus capstone experience (highest senior enrollment); however, many institutions indicated the prevalence of more than one type. Findings on the objectives of the capstone experiences revealed increased critical thinking, analytical, and/or problem-solving skills as the most dominant goals followed by the ability to perform scholarly research, career preparation, professional development, and enhanced written communication skills. The authors acknowledged the intentional approach institutions have taken at planning the goals and objectives for these experiences; however, they noted there is a need for more direct outcome measures. The diversity in the number and type of capstone experiences offered at individual institutions presents additional challenges to outcomes assessment. Despite this, the researchers indicated that this type of assessment is critical in providing an accurate understanding of the direct effect capstone participation has on students. Ultimately, this information will help identify the specific types of capstone experiences that have the most significant impact on students at a particular institution.

Rhodes, T. L., & Agre-Kippenhan, S. (2004, January/February). A multiplicity of learning: Capstones at Portland State University. *Assessment Update, 16*(1), 4-12.

In this article, the authors described the assessment plan associated with a capstone course offered as part of the general education at Portland State University. The evaluation of the six-credit-hour course consisted of authentic assessment in the form of a rubric-evaluated common assignment, student self-report data collected through course evaluations, and an external study examining the educational gains associated with participation in the capstone course. The authors indicated that changes were made to the common assignment and rubric after the initial scores on the assignment were lower than expected. Data from the external study suggested students made educational gains in leadership and communication skills, understanding diverse people and perspectives, and the interest in and desire to volunteer. Based on the assessment experiences tied to this capstone course, the authors suggested assessment measures for these courses be closely aligned with course goals and include multiple measures and strategies to account for the potential range in student learning and characteristics.

Rowles, C. J., Koch, D. C., Hundley, S. P., & Hamilton, S. J. (2004). Toward a model for capstone experiences: Mountaintops, magnets, and mandates. *Assessment Update, 16*(1), 13-15.

This article discussed the Indiana University-Purdue University Indianapolis (IUPUI) initiative to develop a campuswide, curricular, senior capstone experience for all baccalaureate students as one way to show evidence of student learning. Three structures were proposed for the organization of the capstone: mountaintop, magnet, and mandate. The mountaintop was an interdisciplinary approach to the capstone bringing two disciplines together. The magnet was a summative capstone that could focus on research or professional development. The mandate structure allowed students to show competencies and skills required of those in certain professions, such as teaching or nursing. The author noted the discipline should guide pedagogical decisions in capstone development. While a number of challenges to institutional-wide capstones were discussed, faculty involvement and support in the development process are essential.

Sullivan, B. F., & Thomas, S. L. (2007). Documenting student learning outcomes through a research-intensive senior capstone experience: Bring the data together to demonstrate progress. *North American Journal of Psychology, 9*(2), 321-330.

This article explored how the psychology department at Southern Illinois University Edwardsville (SIUE) used a research-intensive senior capstone course to indicate the curriculum resulted in both positive and significant achievement of student learning outcomes. The outcomes were examined using four criteria: (a) articulation and evidence of outcomes, (b) success with regard to outcomes, (c) public dissemination of information about the outcomes, and (d) use of the outcomes for improvement. Under each category, the authors detailed how SIUE practices within the psychology department met the criteria. They concluded by noting data demonstrating learning outcomes can come from a variety of sources and that institutions need to determine the most effective way to find and collect that data. Lastly, they felt faculty participation in the process was key to the overall success of the effort.

CHAPTER 4

Special Populations of Students in Transitions

This chapter summarizes literature related to special populations of students in transition who are either beginning or returning to higher education at a nontraditional age or experiencing college in a different country. These populations include adult learners, student veterans, international students, and study abroad participants. There has been an increase in adult learners (i.e., individuals who are 25 years of age or older) returning to college campuses throughout the United States (Wyatt, 2011). According to the U.S. Census Bureau, there were 6,924,000 adult learners enrolled either part- or full-time in 2008, and that number is projected to rise to 8,198,000 by the year 2017 (National Center for Education Statistics, 2009). Similarly, higher education is seeing a large influx of enrollment from veterans (McBain, 2008), many of whom are returning to civilian life after post-9/11 service and taking advantage of the Post-9/11 Veterans Educational Assistance Act of 2008 (i.e., Post 9/11 GI Bill), which increased existing educational benefits to veterans. The surge in adult learners and veterans (many of whom are also nontraditional-aged) has resulted in a need for institutions to examine various factors and attributes of these special populations in order to serve their unique needs.

Another group with specific needs is student sojourners: U.S. students who study abroad and international students who study at institutions outside of their native countries. These groups are similar in that they both have transitional needs that must be addressed before, during, and upon returning from their experience abroad. However, each group of sojourners also has their own specific issues described in the research below.

Summary of Findings

A common theme found in the research across these special student populations was the significance of interactions with peers, faculty, and staff during the transition process. These interactions can help build a sense of community. For adult learners and veterans, who often felt marginalized or disengaged from fellow students, relationships with faculty and staff provided connections to the campus culture and helped them learn how to navigate institutional policies and procedures. The literature on student veterans especially emphasized their challenge in making meaningful connections with peers, who they often viewed as immature and unable to relate to their military experiences. For student sojourners, high levels of social interaction can help them fit into their new cultures, limit isolation, and reduce levels of culture shock. In addition, this type of engagement can increase English fluency for international students, which is critical in promoting their adjustment. The research also suggests the importance of providing sensitivity training for faculty and staff who are interacting with student sojourners transitioning into or out of a different culture.

Another common theme that arose from the literature is that customized transitional programs are critical to the success of these special populations. For example, orientation programs tailored to their needs, peer mentoring programs, support groups, and coaches (e.g., advisors) can all support these students in their unique transition experiences. For adult learners, accelerated degree programs and strategies to help them balance school with their home life can be useful. Veterans can benefit from more structured programs since transitioning from a highly ordered to a more self-directed environment (i.e., military to academic) can be stressful. Though special orientation programs are important for student sojourners living in a foreign county, the literature emphasized that study abroad participants often need more support in transitioning back into their own culture in order to combat reverse culture shock.

Omissions and Areas of Future Research

Though the research related to student sojourners is fairly robust, there are gaps. A few studies on international students focused on assisting them in preparation for their arrival, but most of the literature centered on helping students take stock of coping resources once they arrived on campus. No research was found that addressed assisting international students with the transition back to their native country. In contrast, some of the research on U.S. students who study abroad examined predeparture issues for this population, but the bulk of the literature focused on re-entry concerns and how institutions can maximize positive outcomes for students upon their return home. Filling in these research gaps would provide a more comprehensive picture of how to support student sojourners at all points of their transition.

On the other hand, the literature on adult learners and student veterans is comparatively sparse. The articles in these sections include primarily qualitative research or program descriptions. Additional research using quantitative methods would broaden the knowledge base for these special populations.

Adult Learners

Bash, L. (2003). Adult learners: *Why they are important to the 21st century college or university. Journal of Continuing Higher Education, 51*(3), 18-26.
The article provided a description of how adult learning-focused programs can serve as an institutional model for higher education in the 21st century. The author began with an exploration of some of the challenges facing adult learners (e.g., lack of institutional support, treatment as second-class students requiring less overhead, limited faculty investment and interaction). Yet, he characterized adult education as being more flexible, responsive, and creative than what is typically offered to traditional-aged students and attributed this to adult learners seeing themselves as consumers seeking direct and practical responses to their needs, often resulting in new *products* (e.g., new courses, certifications, degrees). Bash called this an entrepreneurial approach to education, which encompassed qualities such as risk taking, creativity, innovation, strategic planning, vision, flexibility, and responsiveness, and he argued that institutions must adopt this type of programming to meet the challenges of 21st century education. While adult education has historically employed elements of the entrepreneurial approach, the author noted additional changes must be made (e.g., distance learning, centers for continuing education) to meet the diverse needs of today's students and ensure they participate in lifelong learning. Further, policies that offer the greatest access to learning must be implemented, and institutions should strive to promote access to continuous learning for all students.

Barton, S. (2000). *Investigating the implementation of student orientation in an adult basic education program* (Virginia Adult Education Research Network Practitioner Research Briefs, 1999-2000 Report Series). Richmond, VA: Virginia State Department of Education.
The author examined a new orientation program designed for adult basic education students in 17 classes throughout three rural counties and one city in Virginia. The orientation consisted of instructors using a program guide and spending one hour during five class periods to provide adult students with program information. Six female instructors were interviewed to learn how they implemented the new orientation program in their classes. Through the new

orientation program, they were able to create a comfortable environment by use of dialog. The author learned from the interviews the importance of training instructors on group instruction, assessment, and finding ways to actively involve students in their own learning. It was suggested that instructors have the flexibility to modify the program based on their students' needs.

Deil-Amen, R. (2011). Socio-academic integrative moments: Rethinking academic and social integration among two-year college students in career-related programs. *The Journal of Higher Education, 82*(1), 54-91.
Drawing from data collected through one-on-one interviews and surveys, this study examined the social and academic integration of 238 nontraditional students at two-year institutions. Participants perceived institutional representatives (e.g., trusted faculty, staff, students) as playing an important role in their integration into the institution and contributing to their feelings of confidence and belonging. For African American students in the study, these relationships were of particular importance in helping them make personal and cultural connections with others on the campus. Because the participants were nontraditional students and reported having personal and familial responsibilities, opportunities for interactions on campus were limited. The researchers found that many of the relationships the students discussed developed in class. Even the participants who indicated they had not established any friendships or relationships with peers on campus stated that interactions in the classroom helped them feel more comfortable. Many of these contacts, both in and out of the classroom, were focused around schoolwork. It was also through relationships that students attempted to overcome confusing or intimidating institutional policies or services involving financial aid and advising. Although these experiences could have affected their persistence, the participants acknowledged their relationships with faculty and staff provided them with the guidance and support they needed to successfully navigate institutional policies and procedures.

Ellis, J. R., & Holtrop, S. D. (Eds.) (2012). *In transition: Adult higher education governance in private institutions* (New Directions for Higher Education, No. 159). Hoboken, NJ: John Wiley & Sons.
In this issue composed of multiple case studies, the authors examined how nontraditional adult programs have been integrated into traditional higher education institutions. Motivated by the increased number of adult students pursuing higher education and the unique needs of this population, the chapter authors described how their private colleges and universities responded to the need to create programs for adult learners. Although the focus is on governance

of these programs, attention is paid to the specific needs of faculty, staff, and students affiliated with adult initiatives. For example, one contributor analyzed the existing literature on students' desire to enroll in programs that they consider accessible, both from entry into and out of the program, and found adult students often seek academic programs that will provide accelerated learning opportunities while offering social and academic support. Further, the analysis revealed that many of these programs employed adjunct faculty, and the chapter author indicated a need to devote additional time to hire and train faculty to provide this support to adult learners—something that traditional faculty might not be prepared to do. While administration of adult education programs may be centralized, decentralized, or hybrid (blend of both centralized and decentralized), the authors maintained the approach to these programs should respond directly to the needs of the adult students being served and institutional requirements and structure.

Kasworm, C. (2003). From the adult student's perspective: Accelerated degree programs. In R. J. Wlodkowski & C. E. Kasworm (Eds.), *Accelerated learning for adults: The promise and practice of intensive educational formats* (New Directions for Adult and Continuing Education, No. 97, pp. 17-27). Hoboken, NJ: John Wiley & Sons.

The purpose of this article was to explore accelerated degree programs from the adult learner's perspective. A qualitative research method was used to determine key elements of the adult learner's experience. In addition, the research provided an explanation as to what attracts adult learners to an accelerated degree program. The research concluded that accelerated degree programs were supportive, provided a community of practice, required a specific kind of student identity to be successful, and had paradoxical tensions regarding student learning. A conceptual model of an adult accelerated degree program was created and consisted of three components: (a) adult competence, (b) adult action, and (c) adult work identity. The author concludes that accelerated degree programs represent a learning model grounded in maturity and engagement beyond the classroom.

Merriam, S. (2005). How adult life transitions foster learning and development. In M. A. Wolf (Ed.), *Adulthood: New terrain* (New Directions for Adult and Continuing Education No. 108, pp. 3-13). Hoboken, NJ: John Wiley & Sons.

The article examined transitions in adult life and the relationship of these transitions to learning and development. Transition types were described as well as how adults move through the transition process. Using previous research and transition models from Bridges and Sugarman as a guide, the author explained the importance of reflecting on the transition and ensuring the experience is developmental. The author then examined Mezirow's and Kegan's theories of learning and development to suggest that educators meet the needs of adult learners by promoting developmental change outside their current frame of reference.

Schaefer, J. L. (2010). Voices of older baby boomer students: Supporting their transitions back into college. *Educational Gerontology, 36,* 67-90.

This qualitative study drew on Schlossberg's transition theory to examine the transitional experience of nontraditional students returning to higher education. Interview data were collected and analyzed for recurring themes and ideas. The participants were primarily first-generation college students who chose to pursue higher education to advance in their careers. They discussed choosing their trade when they first entered the workforce and their current desire to receive additional education to pursue a professional career. For many of the students, there were triggers (e.g., children leaving home, loss of job, retirement) that solidified their decision to return to higher education and ultimately to pursue a new or different career. The personal reasons for pursuing higher education were closely linked to career goals, but their status as first-generation students made it more challenging for these students to navigate the transition. This was magnified in their reported need for services, especially academic assistance and personal support. The researcher suggested that development of programs and services, as well as student groups for adult returning students, could assist this population as they are making the transition to higher education.

Sissel, P., Hansman, C., & Kasworm, C. (2001). The politics of neglect: Adult learners in higher education. In C. A. Hansman & P. A. Sissel (Eds.), *Understanding and negotiating the political landscape of adult education* (New Directions for Adult and Continuing Education, No. 91, pp. 17-28), Hoboken, NJ: John Wiley & Sons.

The article examined the lack of privilege of adult learners in higher education from an experiential and empirical perspective by raising questions regarding the limited resources available to serve this population. In addition, the authors explored the neglect of adult learners in higher education through a political lens and the ways in which material, cultural, and symbolic resources influence power and privilege. Concerns focused on the marginalization of both adult learners and the programs serving them (e.g., students not being integrated into the campus culture, programs funded at minimal levels and/or not included in main budgets), as well as the challenge of developing privilege and position for adult learners. The authors proposed that in order to improve the position of adult learners, institutions must promote leadership for all learners that recognizes adult life, adult work, and the role of adults in the academy and community.

Soares, L. (2013). *Post-traditional learners and the transformation of postsecondary education: A manifesto for college leaders.* Retrieved from American Council of Education website: http://www.acenet.edu/news-room/Pages/Post-traditional-Learners-and-the-Transformation-of-Postsecondary-Ed.aspx

This report described the needs of adult learners in the 21st century. The author discussed the importance of increasing the number of Americans who possess academic and applied skills at the postsecondary level. A profile of adult learners was presented, and the challenges educators face delivering substantial learning experiences were explored. Also included was a primer on innovation and a more holistic view of postsecondary education investment. The author examined data from surveys and longitudinal studies to propose three principles as a foundation for achieving better results for adult learners and a catalyst for change: (a) taking a position of leadership in the academy to build a consortium for teaching and learning, (b) rebuilding the definition of postsecondary education from the post-traditional learner out, and (c) being entrepreneurs of a new venture rather than stewards of an existing institution.

Wyatt, L. (2011). Nontraditional student engagement: Increasing adult student success and retention. *The Journal of Continuing Higher Education, 59*(11), 10-20.

The article reviewed findings from a study of nontraditional students and their perceptions of engagement in college, examining those factors that influence nontraditional participation in campus activities. A qualitative approach was used consisting of an online campus climate survey to gather information on the nontraditional student experience on campus, focus groups, and personal interviews. Additionally, participants wrote journal entries of their experiences and plans after graduation. The findings informed the development of a model with the intention of encouraging nontraditional student engagement on college campuses and increasing the number of nontraditional students pursuing higher education. Recommendations for best practices were made to facilitate nontraditional student engagement; these best practices included faculty adapting their teaching methods to serve this special population, developing programs for nontraditional students and their families, and doing a needs assessment of nontraditional students at different stages of their college career.

Student Veterans

DiRamio, D., Ackerman, R., & Mitchell, R. L. (2008). From combat to campus: Voices of student-veterans. *NASPA Journal, 45*(1), 73-102.

In this multicampus study, the researchers used qualitative methods to understand the college transition of 25 student veterans. The interviews were analyzed to identify themes that were applied to Schlossberg's transition theory. Participants described their reasons for joining the military, which included continuing a family tradition, responding to the terrorist attacks on 9/11, and securing the means to pursue higher education. They also discussed the issues or situations encountered as they transitioned to higher education. The majority of participants mentioned peer interactions and fitting in as the most challenging aspects of this part of their transition. Role incongruity between life as a student and life in the military can be magnified by interactions both inside and outside of the classroom. Inappropriate comments and questions about the nature of their military service and professors' antiwar comments in class made student veterans uncomfortable and contributed to their feelings of alienation. The researchers suggested that institutions develop specific programs and support structures for student veterans (e.g., orientation programs, transition coaches, student organizations) and offer training to faculty and staff (especially academic advisors) who interact with these students.

Jones, M. C. (2011). From war zones to classrooms: Student-veterans' perspectives on transition. *The Journal of College Orientation and Transition, 18*(2), 20-32.

Using qualitative methods, this study investigated the college transition of three student veterans. The researcher used Schlossberg's transition theory to examine the unique experiences of the participants, specifically, identifying the role of situation factors, self, support, and strategies on their personal transitions. Although the narratives of each participant were different, they shared similar perceptions of their personal roles in the process of transitioning and the need to belong at their chosen institution. Students indicated personal motivation and the need to improve their status as reasons for pursuing higher education. Although the study participants appeared to be motivated, the researcher suggested it was still critical for institutions to maintain a high level of communication with student veterans because they have a strong desire to belong to the campus community and culture. Further, the researcher suggested creating specific orientation programs for student veterans, as well as designated first-year or transitional seminars for this population. These customized programs could help veterans feel comfortable (as first-time or returning students) because they provide an opportunity to learn about the institution in a safe environment.

Rumann, C. B., & Hamrick, F. A. (2010). Student veterans in transition: Re-enrolling after war zone deployments. *The Journal of Higher Education, 81*(4), 431-458.

Qualitative methods were used to examine the transition of six college students who re-enrolled in higher education after serving in the military. The findings indicated a role incongruity participants faced as they transitioned from members of the military to students. It was through the experience of negotiating these roles that participants realized how different they were from their peers and how much they had changed as a result of their experiences in the military. One area in which participants experienced the most change was in their maturity, which affected their interactions and ability to develop relationships with peers (e.g., a lack of patience for peers who they perceived to be less mature). In other situations, participants described relationship challenges that resulted from identity renegotiation that occurred when they encountered peers who had preconceived notions of veterans.

Ryan, S. W., Carlstrom, A. H., Hughey, K. F., & Harris, B. S. (2011). From boots to books: Applying Schlossberg's model to transitioning American veterans. *NACADA Journal, 31*(1), 55-63.

Drawing on existing research involving student veterans, this study used Schlossberg's transition theory to examine the transition of veterans to higher education and the role advisors play in supporting those students. The authors suggested advisors need to have an understanding of why the student has chosen to pursue higher education because the triggers (leading to the situation or event) and the timing of it are important to the student's ability to be successful. Changes in role can also have an impact on the success of student veterans. Since veterans are often nontraditional students, they might need to develop their academic skills and confidence in a classroom setting. Additionally, transitioning from a structured environment in the military to an environment where they make their own decisions can also lead these students to question their abilities. Advisors can help build student self-confidence by getting student veterans connected with academic resources and by relating this transition (to higher education) to the transition they successfully made when they joined the military. Although these strategies might assist student veterans develop confidence, the researchers indicated it is more challenging for this group to have meaningful interactions with their peers, which was attributed to personal differences often existing between traditional students and student veterans. The authors suggested that developing support groups and student mentors for veterans, as well as dedicated orientation sessions for these students, could assist veterans as they transition to the college or university environment.

Student Sojourners

International Students

Constantine, M. G., Anderson, G., Berkel, L., Caldwell, L., & Utsey, S. (2005). Examining the cultural adjustment experiences of African international college students: A qualitative analysis. *Journal of Counseling Psychology, 52*, 57-66.

The authors explored the adjustment experiences of African international undergraduates studying at a large, mid-Atlantic, predominantly White university in the United States. The 12 participants (two first-year students, three sophomores, four juniors, and three seniors), who hailed from Kenya, Nigeria, and Ghana, were interviewed using a semistructured protocol. The data were coded, and seven final domains were established: (a) presojourn perceptions of the United States, (b) postsojourn perceptions of the United States, (c) cultural adjustment problems in the United States, (d) responses to prejudicial or discriminatory treatment, (e) family and friendship networks, (f) strategies for coping with cultural adjustment problems, and (g) openness to seeking counseling to address cultural adjustment problems. The researchers found that pre- and postsojourn perceptions of the United States were not always congruent, which sometimes led to disappointment, anger, resentment, and culture shock. Given the discrimination some participants experienced, the authors suggested better preparation for the international students as to what they might encounter, as well as outreach and sensitivity training for staff, faculty, and students of the host institution. Though social connections were a prime means of coping for these students, most were not open to seeking professional counseling.

Dao, T. K., Lee, D., & Chang, H. L. (2007). Acculturation level, perceived English fluency, perceived social support level, and depression among Taiwanese international students. *College Student Journal, 41*(2), 287-295.

This study sought to uncover how perceived English fluency, acculturation level, perceived social support, gender, age, and length of stay abroad combine to contribute to the prediction of depression among international students. The sample included 112 Taiwanese international graduate students from a division I university in the southern United States. The participants were asked to complete the Self-Reported Fluency of English Scale, Social Support Questionnaire-Short Form, Suinn-Lew Asian Self-Identity Acculturation Scale, and The Center for Epidemiologic Studies Depression Scale. The data analysis revealed that females, students with lower perceived English fluency, and those with a limited sense of social support were more at risk for depressed feelings. Perceived English fluency mediated the effects of acculturation level on depression for both males and females. The researchers recommend that practitioners stay alert and attend to those students with the identified risk factors, keeping in mind that it is the perception of English fluency and social support that is critical, rather than students' actual support and fluency levels. Educators were advised to facilitate opportunities for social interactions, which can enhance language skills and provide opportunities for the development of a social network. Though this research focused on graduate students, the recommendations might be generalized to international students at all educational levels.

Fritz, M. V., Chin, D., & Demarinis, V. (2008). Stressors, anxiety, acculturation and adjustment among international and North American students. *International Journal of Intercultural Relations, 32*(3), 244-259.

This study compared the adjustment experiences between international and U.S. students, as well as within different cultures of the international student population. The participants were 246 students attending a community college in California, who were divided into three subgroups: Asians (*n* = 71), Europeans (*n* = 40), and permanent U.S. residents (*n* = 97). Thirty-eight additional students did not fit into the regional categorization and were excluded from that portion of the analysis. Data were collected through a questionnaire composed of the Symptom Checklist, the Student Differential Questionnaire, and a section that collected demographic and background information. No significant differences were found between the domestic students and the combined international group. Asian and European students experienced more difficulties with not being able to work and socially related problems. Language posed more challenges for Asian students, while the stress of being separated from family was a bigger challenge for European students.

European, Asian, and domestic students all expressed stress related to finances. The findings suggested that transitional programs for international students must take cultural differences into account, rather than treating these students as one homogeneous group.

Gong, Y. (2003). Goal orientations and cross-cultural adjustment: An exploratory study. *International Journal of Intercultural Relations, 27*(3), 297-305.
This study explored the relationship between goal orientation on the adjustment of international students. The 85 participants were drawn from international students from a large undergraduate class, graduate students from a college of business, and international students who subscribed to the official mailing list for an international student association. The students were mailed a survey containing scales for goal orientation, measures of academic and interaction adjustment, and a section collecting demographic information. The results revealed that learning goal orientation enhanced both academic and interaction adjustment and performance goal orientation enhanced academic adjustment. The researchers suggested goal orientation may impact students differently, depending upon the stage of their sojourn and their country of origin, and recommend future research to explore these ideas.

Kashima, E. S., & Loh, E. (2006). International students' acculturation: Effects of international, conational, and local ties and need for closure. *International Journal of Intercultural Relations, 30*, 471-485.
This study examined the relationship between social ties, acculturation, and need for cognitive closure for 100 Asian international students studying abroad in Melbourne, Australia. The participants completed a questionnaire, which included the Need for Cognitive Closure (NCC) scale, in addition to measuring five acculturation indices: (a) psychological adjustment, (b) sociocultural adjustment, (c) host cultural knowledge, (d) heritage cultural identity, and (e) host university identity. The results revealed that high NCC students had greater adjustment issues, which could be buffered by personal connections with local students and community members. A greater number of international ties tended to predict higher levels of adjustment, and social ties with both international and local students facilitated identification with their host university. Finally, there was a dynamic change in the international students' social identities during their acculturation. The findings suggested that helping international students develop personal connections with other international and host country students can positively promote their cross-cultural adjustment.

Misra, R., Crist, M., & Burant, C. J. (2003). Relationship among life stress, social support, academic stressors, and reactions to stressors of international students in the United States. *International Journal of Stress Management, 10,* 137-157.

This study examined the relationship between life stressors, academic stressors, perceived social support, and reactions to stress among 143 international students at a Midwestern university in the United States. Participants included 62 men and 81 women and were primarily undergraduates (77%) from Africa, Asia, and the Middle East (82%). They completed a questionnaire using the following measures: (a) Index of Life Stress, (b) Student-Life Stress Inventory, and (c) Index of Social Support scale. The results showed that life stress predicted academic stressors and reactions to stressors. The factors that most impacted academic stress were frustration (e.g., from lack of resources, feeling like social outcasts), pressure (e.g., competition, deadlines, work responsibilities), and life changes. Social support, primarily contact with the students' own culture, had a direct and mediating effect between life stress and academic stress. Life stress had a greater effect on academic stress than social support, as the students struggled to adapt to new social values, communication styles, and in some cases, racial discrimination. Though there were no significant differences in academic and life stress by gender, females had higher behavioral, emotional, and psychological reactions to stress. The researchers recommended educators include information about academic support and problem-solving skills for general life stress into orientation and ongoing outreach programs for international students and that programs be tailored for men and women. Additionally, opportunities supporting interactions among both international and domestic students, faculty, and staff should be provided. Finally, the authors suggested cultural sensitivity training for faculty and staff.

Moores, L., & Popadiuk, N. (2011). Positive aspects of international student transitions: A qualitative inquiry. *Journal of College Student Development,* 52(3), 291-306.

This study explored the positive aspects of cross-cultural experiences and the resources that facilitate this transition. The qualitative design combined the Critical Incident Technique and positive psychology. Interviews conducted with seven international students (five graduates and two undergraduates) revealed 134 critical incidents, which were organized into eight categories: (a) growth and/or change, (b) social support or building relationships with peers, (c) learning to navigate the host culture, (d) enjoyable activities outside of schoolwork, (e) previous experiences or preparation, (f) supportive faculty and staff, (g) persevering through hard times, and (h) sense of belonging. The researchers found that connecting with others to build a sense of meaningful community, maintaining a connection to one's native culture and family, embracing the process of adaption to a new culture with flexibility and openness, and discovering and tapping into individual strengths helped to facilitate the cross-cultural transition. They concluded that adequate and relevant support from the university community is critical to the success of this student population.

Mori, C. (2000). Addressing the mental health concerns of international students. *Journal of Counseling and Development, 78*(2), 137-144.

The unique mental health concerns of international students, how that might impact their adjustment to another country and academic system, and strategies for counseling services to address these concerns were explored in this study. The author described the sources of stress for international students as they transition and adapt to a new educational and social environment, including language barriers, cultural gaps, challenges with interpersonal relations, and financial difficulties. The article also described how these stressors could manifest themselves in international students, as well as the resistance of this population to seek professional counseling services. Culturally responsive practices and processes for mental health professionals were presented, including proactive, educational, and collaborative approaches that increase the visibility and accessibility of services while attempting to reduce the stigma associated with them. The author suggested that stress management techniques, assertive communication skills, effective study skills, and career and life planning are the skills that will most benefit international students in making a successful cross-cultural adjustment.

O'Reilly, A., Ryan, D., & Hickey, T. (2010). The psychological well-being and sociocultural adaptation of short-term international students in Ireland. *Journal of College Student Development, 51*(5), 584-598.

This study examined how short-term international students adapted to life in Ireland, how this adaption played out over time, and how it compared to the experiences of the host students. Participants included 51 students (90% undergraduate) from a variety of different countries who were participating in a short-term, cross-cultural program in Ireland and 44 Irish students who served as a control group. The students were surveyed at different points throughout the program on measures of social support, loneliness, college-related stress, psychological distress, and sociocultural adaption. The results revealed that the international students experienced higher levels of social support and lower levels of college-related stress and loneliness than Irish students. The researchers posited that social support, the fact that they lived with other international students on campus, and their high level of English fluency may have buffered any negative effects. Further, Irish students may have been under greater academic stress than the international students, who did not have as many academic responsibilities. Students also reported high levels of sociocultural adaption difficulties; however, these adjustment issues decreased over time, while they reported that levels of social support increased over time. Such sociocultural adjustment issues could be addressed via pre-arrival orientation programs and postarrival support. Further, special-interest housing for international students could also ease the transition for this population, although some researchers have questioned that approach because it discourages interaction with other populations of students.

Poyrazli, S., Arbona, C., Bullington, R., & Pisecco, S. (2001). Adjustment issues of Turkish college students studying in the United States. *College Student Journal, 35(1), 52-62.*

The self-reported adjustment levels of Turkish college students studying in the United States were examined through the following lenses: age, gender, marital status, years spent in the United States, recipient of a government scholarship, English proficiency, and socioeconomic status. The participants were 79 Turkish undergraduate and graduate international students (27% female, 73% male) who completed both a demographic questionnaire and the Inventory of Student Adjustment Strain. Those who did not receive a scholarship reported fewer adjustment issues than the comparison group. The results also revealed that younger students had a higher level of English reading and writing proficiency. This suggested a greater focus needs to be placed on helping non-traditional-aged students adjust. Academic resources should be visibly promoted for students who may need to improve their English proficiency and for those who may feel pressure to maintain a certain GPA in order to qualify for a scholarship.

Poyrazli, S., & Grahame, K. M. (2007). Barriers to adjustment: Needs of international students within a semi-urban community. *Journal of Instructional Psychology, 34*(1), 28-45.

Using an ecological framework, the authors examined the academic and social adjustment issues of international students. The setting was a semi-urban, primarily commuter college in the United States that only enrolled junior, senior, and graduate students. The 15 participants (three females, 12 males) represented different nationalities and included both graduate students and undergraduates. They were interviewed in four focus groups using a semistructured format. The researchers found the students experienced multiple barriers to their participation in their academic and social communities, particularly during their initial transition after arriving in the United States. These barriers included managing housing, transportation, and immigration documents; understanding American students and professors; participating in class; navigating the health care system; and dealing with discrimination, communication issues, and social interaction, particularly with other Americans. The authors suggested more support for the initial transition, such as better quality information about the university and surrounding area, transportation assistance (e.g., shuttle or pick-up service), and housing assistance (e.g., temporary housing services, household merchandise donation programs). Further, they recommended increased social support through peer mentoring, programs that integrate international and domestic students, and better work opportunities.

Ragouzeos, Z., & Wais, M. (2012). Easing the transition for international students: Practical ways to ensure a smooth adjustment. *NASPA Leadership Exchange, 9*(4), 10-15.

The purpose of the article was to address the recruitment of international students and the challenges they face once enrolled. The authors shared how adjustment woes and cultural differences prevent international students from seeking assistance from campus resources, in particular mental health care. Five institutional programs at New York University were highlighted, including a health and mental health hotline, depression screening and counseling, walk-in counseling, counseling at satellite schools and campuses, and a required campus-life orientation program. The authors stressed the importance of incorporating international students into every aspect of university life and suggested creating an affirmative agenda to provide engagement opportunities for international students inside and outside of the classroom. Further, it was recommended scholars and practitioners pay special attention to the mental and overall health of international students.

Toyokawa, T., & Toykowa, N. (2002). Extracurricular activities and the adjustment of Asian international students: A study of Japanese students. *International Journal of Intercultural Relations, 26,* 363-379.

This study explored the relationship between the extracurricular involvement of Japanese students studying in the United States and the students' academic involvement, psychological health, social support, and use of leisure time. Participants were 85 undergraduates (41 males, 44 females) who were engaged in a 10-month, study abroad program. Data were collected using a survey administered approximately nine months into the program. The findings showed higher levels of engagement in extracurricular activities were positively associated with life satisfaction, academic involvement, and the perception of benefits from both academic and extracurricular activities. However, those students in the high-engagement group did not report higher levels of psychological adjustment, social support, and active use of leisure time compared to those in the low-engagement group. Given the reciprocal relationship of academic and extracurricular engagement, the researchers recommended educators make efforts to understand the preferences, interests, and needs of international students to best channel their energies into appropriate out-of-class experiences.

Wilton, L., & Constantine, M. G. (2003). Length of residence, cultural adjustment difficulties, and psychological distress symptoms in Asian and Latin American international college students. *Journal of College Counseling*, 6, 177-186.

This study examined the impact of length of residence and psychological distress on the adjustment of international college students. The participants included 190 Asian and Latin American international students attending a predominantly White university in the northeastern United States. The students completed a survey packet consisting of the Cultural Adjustment Difficulties checklist, a general psychological distress checklist, and a demographic questionnaire. Their Test of English as a Foreign Language (TOEFL) score was also requested to ensure they were proficient enough in English to participate in the study. The results revealed that Latin American students reported significantly higher levels of distress than their Asian counterparts. Shorter length of stay in the United States, higher acculturative distress, and intercultural competence concerns were associated with higher levels of psychological distress for both groups. The authors recommended counseling personnel develop culturally sensitive outreach programs that validate these students' native cultures and help them develop bicultural competence.

Yan, K., & Berliner, D. C. (2011). An examination of individual level factors in stress and coping processes: Perspectives of Chinese international students in the United States. *Journal of College Student Development*, 52(5), 523-542.

The levels of stress, coping, and general acculturation of 18 Chinese international graduate students (10 females, eight males) who were studying at a large, public university in the southwestern United States were examined in this study. Each participant was interviewed for approximately one hour using a semistructured interview format. Data were analyzed and categorized using Berry's Stress-Coping Framework, from which two broad categories emerged: (a) factors prior to acculturation (e.g., age, gender, major, expectation, knowledge, skills) and (b) factors during acculturation (e.g., length of stay, acculturation strategies, coping strategies, social support). These data could be used to inform predeparture information, orientation programs, and ongoing acculturation activities for international students.

Yeh, C. J., & Inose, M. (2003). International students' reported English fluency, social support satisfaction, and social connectedness as predictors of acculturative stress. *Counseling Psychology Quarterly, 16*(1), 15-28.

This research focused on how age, gender, self-reported English language fluency, social connectedness, and social support satisfaction predicted acculturation stress for 359 international students. The sample of undergraduates and graduate students included 60% women and 40% men from 77 unique countries representing four primary geographic regions. Surveys were distributed to the participants at international club and organization meetings and included the following measures: (a) a demographic questionnaire, (b) Acculturative Stress Scale for International Students, (c) Social Connectedness Scale, and the (d) Social Support Questionnaire-Short Form. The results revealed students with higher reported English language fluency and those from Europe experienced lower levels of acculturation stress than students with lower fluency levels and those from Asia, Africa, and Latin or Central America. Higher levels of social connectedness and social support network satisfaction predicted lower levels of acculturation stress. The researchers recommended the development of programs that build community and foster social interaction for international students, such as peer programs matching international and domestic students.

Zhao, C. M., Kuh, G. D., & Carini, R. M. (2005). A comparison of international student and American student engagement in effective educational practices. *Journal of Higher Education, 76*(2), 209-231.

This research used data from the National Survey of Student Engagement (NSSE) to compare the levels of engagement of international and American college students in their exposure to effective educational practices. A total of 175,000 students from 317 four-year institutions completed the NSSE; 4% of the total sample ($n = 2,780$) identified as international students, and of those, 47% were first-year students and 53% were seniors. The researchers assessed eight measures of engagement and four measures of student self-reported outcomes: (a) academic challenge; (b) active and collaborative learning; (c) student-faculty interaction; (d) supportive campus environment; (e) diversity experiences; (f) community service; (g) computer technology use; (h) time spent socializing and relaxing; and (i) student-reported gains in general education, personal and social development, job-related skills, and student satisfaction. The results revealed international students do not differ from their American peers by their senior year in their level of engagement, with the exception of two areas. International students presented higher gains in personal and social development and general education, which is not surprising given the constant opportunities for growth and knowledge acquisition that living in a foreign country presents. Further, international student were less engaged in community service, an activity that may not resonate with them, unless community is presented in more global terms. The researchers suggested educators compare these data to the experiences of international students on their own campuses to determine which mixes of students, curricular requirements, and campus cultures will help students in making the most successful transition to college life in the United States. For example, the impacts of early socialization experiences (e.g., orientation), housing arrangements, and the number of international students on campus all merit further investigation. Other implications for those who advise and educate international students were discussed.

Study Abroad Students

Gaw, K. F. (2000). Reverse culture shock in students returning from overseas. *International Journal of Intercultural Relations, 24*(1), 83-104.

The re-entry experiences of 66 overseas-experienced American college students were examined to determine if reverse culture shock resulted in perceived problems and affected the willingness to seek help or services the students used. A re-entry packet, including the Reverse Shock Scale and Personal Problems Inventory, was mailed to the participants, who represented all undergraduate class levels. The results revealed returnees who experienced higher levels of reverse culture shock were more likely to report personal adjustment problems and shyness than those who experienced lower levels of reverse culture shock. Both groups were equally likely to see a counselor for their concerns, though those reporting higher levels of reverse culture shock were less likely to use student support services. The researcher recommended college counseling centers provide both individual services and programming for the returning student population, including cultural orientation, discussion groups, social functions, and opportunities to become involved with international student groups.

Gonyea, R. M. (2008, November). *The impact of study abroad on senior year engagement.* Paper presented at the annual meeting of the Association for the Study of Higher Education, Jacksonville, FL.

This study used longitudinal data from the National Survey of Student Engagement (NSSE), administered at 140 institutions, to examine how study abroad impacted engagement in the senior year, as well as student's self-reported gains, after controlling for student and institutional characteristics. First-year student responses from 2004 were matched with senior responses from 2007, resulting in 2,311 matches with seniors who had studied abroad. The data revealed study abroad participants were more engaged than their peers in two deep forms of learning: integrative reflective learning and diversity experiences. They were also more likely to report making progress in their college learning and their personal and social development. The researcher used these findings to make recommendations for faculty members and administrators to help successfully reintegrate study abroad participants into their home campus and mitigate the stress of reverse culture shock. For example, using these students' observations within classroom discussions and assignments can encourage study abroad participants to reflect and process their experiences while enhancing the learning environment for all students. The author also recommended that study abroad advisors communicate the needs of returning students to faculty and advisors so that they have a better understanding of the challenges these students face and what might be beneficial to their reacculturation process.

Kitsantas, A. (2004). Studying abroad: The role of college students' goals on the development of cross-cultural skills and global understanding. *College Student Journal*, 38, 441-452.

This study examined the relationship between study abroad, student goals, and the development of cross-cultural skills and global understanding. Participants included 232 college students enrolled in study abroad programs in England, Italy, Greece, France, and Spain. The sample consisted of 112 sophomores, 63 juniors, 30 first-year students, and 25 seniors. A pretest, consisting of the Cross-Cultural Adaptability Inventory (CCAI), Study Abroad Goals Scale, and a personal data section, was administered prior to their study abroad experience. Upon their return from study abroad, the participants completed a posttest (i.e., the CCAI and the Global Perspective Survey). Among the findings, the researcher learned that students' goals to study abroad predicted improvement in their cross-cultural skills and global understanding. Specifically, more improvements were found among those students whose goals were to improve cross-cultural and academic competence, compared to those who wanted to participate in study abroad for social reasons. Given the critical role that goals play on the development of cross-cultural skills, the researcher recommended a predeparture program for study abroad participants with an intent to develop and reinforce goals promoting cultural learning and sensitivity. She suggested focusing students on goals more likely to positively impact their development and study abroad experience, which can help create a smoother transition and increase the likelihood students would persist in the program.

Ryan, M. E., & Twibell, R. S. (2000). Concerns, values, stress, coping, health and educational outcomes of college students who studied abroad. *International Journal of Intercultural Relations, 24*, 409-435.

The purpose of this longitudinal study was to examine the cross-cultural adaptation and learning experiences of study abroad students by looking at (a) the nature of stressful situations experienced; (b) the relationships among stress, coping, and health; and (c) educational outcomes. The participants were 154 American college students who had studied outside the United States for at least one semester. Data were collected at three different points (i.e., prior to their study abroad experience, two months into their time abroad, and upon their return to the United States) using a values and goals questionnaire, the BT Challenge Instrument, the Jalowiec Coping Scale, and a medical outcomes survey. The results showed the primary concerns of the students included those related to personal relationships and fitting into a new society, academic achievement, communication and language skills, personal adjustment, health and safety, and bureaucratic procedures. The students became more prosocial in values orientation as the study abroad experience progressed. Further, most students perceived their experience as only slightly threatening and moderately to highly challenging. Finally, the students dealt with their challenges ineffectively, as they used few coping strategies. The researchers suggested that developing orientation programs addressing the primary concern areas for students and providing a means for developing effective coping strategies would help promote successful cross-cultural adjustment for study abroad students.

Souders, B. V. (2006). Now that I am home, who am I? Renegotiating American identity among returned study abroad participants. *LLC Review*, 6(1), 22-41.

This qualitative study examined the reinterpreted identity of study abroad students after their return to the United States. Participants were 12 undergraduates at a medium-sized, public university in the mid-Atlantic region who had completed a one-semester international study abroad program. Data were collected through one-hour semistructured interviews. Common themes included (a) embracing a willingness to adapt another country's national identity, (b) facing challenges of being American, (c) deriving pleasure in being confused for another nationality, (d) perceiving themselves as different from their prestudy abroad self and different from their study abroad peers, (e) seeing the experience as an idealized adventure, and (f) experiencing both negative and positive stereotyping from the host nationals. Upon their return to the United States, all students expressed feeling different from not only their peers and family members but also Americans in general, suggesting a renegotiated sense of identity. Though not explicitly stated, the findings have implications for advisors, counselors, faculty members, and other student affairs staff who will interact with these students upon their re-entry into the country. Students could benefit from programs, interactions, classroom discussions, and assignments that allowed them to process their experiences and make meaning of this new sense of self.

Wielkiewicz, R. M., & Turkowski, L. W. (2010). Reentry issues upon returning from study abroad programs. *Journal of College Student Development, 51*(6), 649-664.

This study used quantitative data collected from a survey examining the potential effect of study abroad participation on the interpersonal relationships of students. Among the 669 participants, 36.2% had studied abroad. Based on findings from previous studies, the researchers expected to find elevated levels of anxiety and decreased personal or romantic relationships; however, current data suggested that study abroad participation did not have a significant negative impact on relationships with others. Students who studied abroad reported more skepticism about their home culture, higher rates of alcohol consumption, and higher academic workload upon their return home. There were nascent findings indicating gender differences, including female study abroad participants reporting greater levels of stress than male participants, which the authors suggested is an area for further investigation. Additionally, the researchers recommended that professionals working with study abroad programs consider developing opportunities (e.g., focus groups) for students returning from study abroad to interact with other re-entering students.

REFERENCES

Allen, I. E., Seaman, J., Lederman, D., & Jaschik, S. (August, 2012). *Digital faculty: Professors, teaching and technology, 2012* (Inside Higher Ed and Babson Survey Research Group Report). Retrieved from http://babson.qualtrics.com/SE/?SID=SV_bJHd6VpmahG2NGB

Evans, N. J., Forney, D. S., Guido, F. M., Patton, L. D., & Renn, K. A. (2010). *Student development in college: Theory, research, and practice* (2nd ed.). San Francisco, CA: Jossey-Bass.

Feldman, K. A., & Newcomb, T. M. (1969). *The impact of college on students, Vol. I: An analysis of four decades of research*. San Francisco, CA: Jossey-Bass.

Freedman, M. B. (1956). The passage through college. *Journal of Social Issues, 12*(4), 13-28.

Gardner, J. N., Pattengale, J., & Schreiner, L. A. (2000). Summary and recommendations. In L. A. Schreiner & J. Pattengale (Eds.), *Visible solutions for invisible students: Helping sophomores succeed* (Monograph No. 31, pp. 89-93). Columbia, SC: University of South Carolina, National Resource Center for The First-Year Experience & Students in Transition.

Gardner, J. N., Van der Veer, G., & Associates. (1998). *The senior year experience: Facilitating integration, reflection, closure and transition*. San Francisco, CA: Jossey-Bass.

Goodman, J., Schlossberg, N. K., & Anderson, M. L. (2006). *Counseling adult students in transition: Linking theory with practice* (3rd ed.). New York, NY: Springer.

Koch, A. K., Foote, S. M., Hinkle, S. E., Keup, J., & Pistilli, M. D. (Eds.). (2007). *The first-year experience in American higher education: An annotated bibliography* (Monograph No. 3, 4th ed.). Columbia, SC: University of South Carolina, National Resource Center for The First-Year Experience and Students in Transition.

Lemons, J. L., & Richmond, D. R. (1987). A developmental perspective of sophomore slump. *NASPA Journal, 24*(3), 15-19.

Margolis, G. (1976). *Unslumping our sophomores: Some clinical observations and strategies. Journal of American College Health, 25*, 133-136.

McBain, L. (2008). *When Johnny [or Janelle] comes marching home: National, state and institutional efforts in support of veteran's education.* Retrieved from http://www.aascu.org/uploadedFiles/AASCU/Content/Root/PolicyAndAdvocacy/PolicyPublications/08b_perspectives(1).pdf

Moos, R. H., & Tsu, V. (1976). Human competence and coping: An overview. In R. H. Moos (Ed.), *Human adaptation: Coping with life crises* (pp. 3-16). Lexington, MA: Heath.

National Center for Education Statistics. (2009). *Digest of education statistics, 2008* (NCES 2009-020). Washington, DC: U.S. Department of Education.

Schlossberg, N. K. (1981). A model for analyzing human adaptation to transition. *The Counseling Psychologist, 9*, 2-18.

Schlossberg, N. K. (1984). *Counseling adults in transition.* New York, NY: Springer Publishing Company.

Tinto, V. (2012). *Completing college: Rethinking institutional action.* Chicago, IL: University of Chicago Press.

Wyatt, L. G. (2011). Nontraditional student engagement: Increasing adult student success and retention. *Journal of Continuing Higher Education, 59*(1), 10-20.

INDEX

C

G

H

I

J

K

N

R

S

V

W

Y

Z

Acknowledgments

We would be remiss if we did not take this opportunity acknowledge the tremendous support we received from our families, both personal and professional. Specifically, we would like to thank our partners, spouses, and children: Jason Plafcan; Robert, Jabari, and Zoe Miles; Kelly, Gwendolyn, and Theodore Pistilli; Kevin Kranzow, as well as Kieran and Karissa; Janelle, Frederick, Claude, Lillian, Ayesha, and Sydney Simmons; and Sherri-Ann, Caleb, Maya, and Kayla Terry. We would also like to thank the wonderful and talented editorial staff at the National Resource Center, especially Toni Vakos, Tracy Skipper, Jennifer Keup, and Allison Minsk. We are also indebted to our dear friend and professional colleague Drew Koch, who helped us begin this journey, as well as the interlibrary loan staff in the Humanities, Social Science, and Education Library at Purdue University.

Last, and certainly not least, we would like to recognize the myriad college students in transition with whom we work. You truly inspire us and make us want to broaden the collective understanding of who you are and the unique transitions you experience.

About the Authors

Stephanie M. Foote is an associate professor of education in the Department of First-Year and Transition Studies Programs at Kennesaw State University. Before her arrival at Kennesaw in 2011, she was the administrator for academic success and first-year programs at the University of South Carolina Aiken. Foote is a past recipient of the NODA Outstanding Research Award for her dissertation study of the perceived effects of first-year seminar participation on the experience of students in their first semester of college. She has published and presented on her research involving college students in transition and has developed and taught online courses on fostering the success of first-year students. Foote has been a commission chair for the ACPA-College Student Educators International Commission on Admissions, Orientation, and First Year Experience. She currently is on the editorial board for the *Journal of Student Affairs Research and Practice* and is the editor for the *Journal of College Orientation and Transition*.

Sara E. Hinkle has more than 17 years of experience promoting college student engagement and success in various areas of student affairs. She is the assistant vice president for Student Affairs at West Chester University and was formerly the associate dean for Student and Community Development at Hofstra University, where she oversaw student leadership and activities; multicultural education and programming; and services and programs for new students, commuters, and international students. Hinkle earned a PhD in higher education from Indiana University Bloomington, an MS in counseling from Georgia State University, and a BA in psychology from Gettysburg College. Among the more than 50 national presentations and publications to her credit, she is a co-editor of the *The First-Year Experience in American Higher Education: An Annotated Bibliography* (4th ed., 2007) and a contributing researcher, editor, and author of *Student Success in College: Creating Conditions That Matter* (2005, 2010). Hinkle is an active member of ACPA-College Student Educators International and a past-chair of the ACPA Commission for Admissions, Orientation, and First Year Experience.

Jeannine Kranzow has a BA from Pepperdine University, an MA from California Lutheran University, and a PhD in higher education from Indiana University Bloomington. She is an assistant professor in College Counseling and Student Development at Azusa Pacific University. Kranzow has published articles and presented research on various topics in higher education, including college student transition; graduate-program marketing; and impacts of various curricular structures on student critical thinking, motivation, and self-direction. She has administrative experience in academic advising, career services, and women's affairs. Kranzow is involved with ACPA-College Student Educators International and the International Society for Self-Directed Learning (ISSDL).

Matthew D. Pistilli is a research scientist for Teaching and Learning Technologies at Purdue University. For more than 13 years, he has focused on creating and assessing conditions and environments that positively impact college student success. Over his career, Pistilli has worked with summer bridge programs, residence life, learning communities, orientation programming, Supplemental Instruction, low-income student scholarship and support programming, and the application of data in efforts to increase student success. He has presented numerous times on these topics. After studying the impact of learning communities on women in STEM majors for his doctoral dissertation, Pistilli began examining the intersection of technology and student success. Currently, he is as the principal investigator and project director for an initiative funded by the Bill and Melinda Gates Foundation looking at the process for building capacity for using analytics at eight institutions around the United States in an effort to impact student success. He has published on learning analytics, learning communities, college seniors, and low-income student success programming, and has co-edited two annotated bibliographies on the transitions to and through college. Pistilli holds a BA in Spanish and psychology from Southwest Minnesota State University, as well as two graduate degrees from Purdue University: an MS in Education in College Student Affairs and Counseling and a PhD in Higher Education Administration.

La'Tonya Rease Miles is the director of the Academic Resource Center at Loyola Marymount University, where she provides academic support to students in transition. Miles also teaches part-time for the Department of English and is director of the First To Go program. She earned her PhD in English from UCLA and has presented and written about sophomore success programs, mentoring students in undergraduate research, and preparing students for graduate school. Her current research interests include narratives about the first-generation college experience and the hidden curriculum in higher education.

Janelle G. Simmons is the director of New Student Services at North Carolina Central University. She received her BA in Social Sciences Interdisciplinary and MA in Social Work with a specialization in Student Community Development from Stony Brook University. She is currently a doctoral student pursuing her EdD in Higher Education and Adult Learning from Walden University. Simmons has 13 years of experience in student development, including residential life and transition programming. She also taught the first-year seminar and a course on academic integrity. Simmons is a member of ACPA-College Student Educators International and was the chair of the ACPA Commission for Admissions, Orientation, and First Year Experience from 2005 to 2007. She also was the cochair of the Multi-Ethnic Network for NODA-Association for Orientation, Transition, and Retention in Higher Education.